**2ND EDITION**

# BACKROADS OF
# FLORIDA

## ALONG THE BYWAYS TO BREATHTAKING LANDSCAPES AND QUIRKY SMALL TOWNS

# PAUL M. FRANKLIN & NANCY MIKULA

VOYAGEUR
PRESS

Quarto is the authority on a wide range of topics.

Quarto educates, entertains and enriches the lives of our readers—enthusiasts and lovers of hands-on living.

www.quartoknows.com

Acquiring Editor: Todd Berger
Project Manager: Madeleine Vasaly
Art Director: James Kegley
Design and Layout: Diana Boger

First edition published in 2009 by Voyageur Press, an imprint of Quarto Publishing Group USA Inc., 400 First Avenue North, Suite 400, Minneapolis, MN 55401 USA. Telephone: (612) 344-8100 Fax: (612) 344-8692. This edition published in 2016.

quartoknows.com
Visit our blogs at quartoknows.com

Voyageur Press titles are also available at discounts in bulk quantity for industrial or sales-promotional use. For details contact the Special Sales Manager at Quarto Publishing Group USA Inc., 400 First Avenue North, Suite 400, Minneapolis, MN 55401 USA.

10 9 8 7 6 5 4 3 2 1

ISBN: 978-0-7603-5036-2

Library of Congress Cataloging-in-Publication Data

Names: Franklin, Paul M., author. | Mikula, Nancy, 1947- photographer.
Title: Backroads of Florida : along the byways to breathtaking landscapes &
    quirky small towns / Paul M. Franklin and Nancy Mikula.
Description: Second edition. | Minneapolis, MN : Voyageur Press, 2016. |
    Series: Backroads | "First edition published in 2009 by Voyageur Press, an
    imprint of Quarto Publishing Group USA Inc."--Title page verso.
Identifiers: LCCN 2016019276 | ISBN 9780760350362 (paperback)
Subjects: LCSH: Florida--Tours. | Scenic byways--Florida--Guidebooks. |
    Automobile travel--Florida--Guidebooks. | BISAC: TRAVEL / United States /
    South / South Atlantic (DC, DE, FL, GA, MD, NC, SC, VA, WV). | TRAVEL /
    Pictorials (see also PHOTOGRAPHY / Subjects & Themes / Regional). | TRAVEL
    / United States / General.
Classification: LCC F309.3 .F73 2016 | DDC 917.5904--dc23
LC record available at https://lccn.loc.gov/2016019276

**Frontis:** Low tide at the Florida Keys Islands. View from West Summerland Key. *Shutterstock/ liseykina*

**Title page:** Brilliant white sand and emerald waves are hallmarks of Florida's beaches. This beautiful strand is in Gulf Island National Seashore near Pensacola.

**Contents, left:** Alligators can often be found lying on wetland banks in Florida with their mouths agape. Scientists believe this helps them regulate their body temperature.

**Contents, right:** A brilliantly colored macaw watches people go by from his enclosed perch on Sanibel Island in southern Florida.

Printed in China

# DEDICATION

This book is dedicated to our fabulous sisters:
Pam, Barb, Marie, and Kay.
You have allowed us to amuse you with our
lifestyle. You have encouraged us with kind words.
And most of all, you have shared your laughter, friendship,
and love with us through all the times, good and bad.
We cherish you all very much.

# ACKNOWLEDGMENTS

OVER THE MONTHS that we researched and traveled the backroads of Florida, we were constantly amazed at how much help we received, often from people we barely knew. There is no way we can thank them all in this small space, but we will try to name a few. Thanks to the wonderful folks at Stuart Newman Associates for fabulous assistance in the Florida Keys. And likewise to the excellent team at Florida's Historic Coast for their excellent assistance in St. Augustine. To all those who opened the doors to their interesting worlds, especially Robert of Robert Is Here exotic fruit stand, Howard Solomon and family at the unique Solomon's Castle, Jack Rudloe at the Gulf Specimen Marine Laboratory in Panacea, and Chris Pendleton and Lisa Wilson at Edison Ford Winter Estates, a big thanks. Our gratitude also goes out to all the national and state park personnel who helped us learn more about Florida's incredible parks. And finally, to all those who labor long and hard, and often with too little recognition, to preserve and protect Florida's historic and wild places for future generations, you have our deepest appreciation and our prayers.

# CONTENTS

# INTRODUCTION

When we started researching and writing this book, there was one question we were asked most: does Florida even have backroads? It's an understandable query, as many who visit the Sunshine State experience it by rocketing along interstates to Orlando or the latest beach resort. However, for those who know and love Florida's tens of thousands of miles of two-lane blacktops, posing such a question is like asking if the Rockies have mountains.

In fact, the minute you get off the interstate and head into the lesser-known regions of the state, you'll find wonderful places filled with stunning natural beauty, incredible history, and true once-in-a-lifetime experiences. Want to snorkel with a manatee or get up close and personal with a sixteen-foot alligator? Want to hunt for sunken treasure or watch a rocket blast off for the stars? This is the place to do it. Beyond the famous Florida of sand and sun, you'll

discover the state's rich seafaring history and awe-inspiring wilderness, places where cowboy legends and tropical mysteries abound. The backroad roamers know the secret: whichever flavor of Florida you seek, there is a scenic byway or a two-lane road to take you there. But where exactly do Florida's backroads and byways lead? Of course, into the heart of the wet, wild, all-natural Florida Everglades, where tranquil estuaries, horizonless marshes, and darkly inviting swamps are home to alligators gliding silently through mirror-black waters. The roughly 1.5 million acres here are adventure central, where you can hike hidden trails through ancient forests of pine and moss-draped oaks; paddle your kayak through tidal wetlands teeming with herons, egrets, and roseate spoonbills; or drift along black-water rivers where mighty cypress trees festooned with delicate orchids reach from the dark waters to the sky.

Florida's backroads also lead into the heartland, a little-explored world of rolling green hills, lush citrus orchards,

Left: **This patriotically painted classic Ford pickup is the first thing that greets visitors at the Tallahassee Automobile Museum.**

Opposite: **A lone palm tree leans as if longing to be closer to the beautiful beach on Jupiter Island.**

and sparkling lakes, where quarter horses run in white-fenced meadows and park-like cattle ranches line miles of shady byways. They pass through charming small towns, such as Mount Dora, Madison, and Lake Wales, which offer timeless storefront main streets lined with craft and antique shops, galleries, and ice cream parlors. And no doubt about it, Florida's backroads eventually lead one and all to the magnificent kingdom of kitsch. No place can equal the Sunshine State in serving up heaping help-ings of roadside silliness and eccentricity. Whether it's the monumental sculpture-filled whimsy of aluminum-plated Solomon's Castle in central Florida or the quirky humor (not to mention juice-dripping-down-your-chin delicious-ness) you'll find at the Robert Is Here exotic fruit stand, Florida is full of the weird and wonderful. In spite of a pervasive belief that every inch of Florida's coast has been developed, Florida's backroads do lead to untamed stretches of sand and sea, where you can drive for miles enjoying views of turquoise surf, wind-tossed shoreline palms, or quiet estuaries alive with birds and wildlife. At places such as Canaveral National Seashore, Big Talbot Island, or Lovers Key, you can stroll barefoot along seem-ingly endless stretches of sun-warmed sandy surf line, where gulls float effortlessly through the air and the sea oats sway gently along vast stretches of empty dunes. Head out on Florida's backroads and you'll discover a world of history and legends, of heroes and villains—from pirates and adventurers to fierce native warriors. You'll explore St. Augustine, where an ancient stone fortress defends the oldest town in America and ships still set their course on stormy nights by a haunted lighthouse, and Orchid Island, where pieces of eight still wash ashore from a treasure fleet that sank three centuries ago. Ultimately, you'll find the near-mythical realm of "Old Florida"—that place of unique and astonishing nature, Southern charm and grace, road-side weirdness and quirky intrigue—is alive and well.

You'll find it out there on the rambling country roads, the oak-shaded lanes, and timeless byways of the state that, perhaps more than any other, represents the promise of dreams come true.

**The day's last rays of sun strike a stand of cypress in a wetland somewhere in north central Florida.**

# PART I
# SOUTHERN FLORIDA

A great egret stands at the edge of a tidal marsh, waiting patiently for his dinner to swim by.
The Anhinga Trail is one of the best bird-watching areas in the Everglades National Park.

SOUTHERN FLORIDA serves up such a rich and spicy stew of stunning natural places, exotic tropical culture, and uniquely Floridian strangeness that one longtime resident noted "the farther south you go, the weirder it gets!"

Otherworldly attractions, such as the beautiful Florida Keys and ancient Everglades, mingle with all forms of roadside kitsch here. In the once-impenetrable Everglades, visitors can find astounding numbers of rare and fascinating plants, birds, and animals found nowhere else in the United States. Skimming airboats lead to hidden deep-water expanses where alligators wait with prehistoric patience for their prey. Farther west is the shadowy and mysterious Big Cypress National Preserve. True to its name, this reserve protects vast black-water swamps dominated by some of the largest cypress trees in the United States.

Along Florida's Gulf Coast, the landscape becomes decidedly more urban, especially around Fort Meyers. But you'll also find charming laid-back islands that offer inviting sun-warmed sand beaches, small roads for touring, and some of the planet's best shell collecting.

In Miami, the remarkable story of Florida's evolution in the twentieth century is just part of the story that waits to be discovered in some of the city's historic hotspots, including Little Havana, the romantic mansion and gardens of Vizcaya, and the ultrahip Art Deco district in South Beach.

South of Miami, Homestead and Florida City offer a tasty slice of old-time Florida surrounded by great expanses of rich farmlands that yield mangoes, pineapples, and citrus of many varieties. Here, too, are some of Florida's most unusual attractions, such as the puzzling Coral Castle, built single-handedly by a tiny Latvian immigrant to commemorate his unrequited love.

Florida City is the gateway to that most Floridian of all places: the Florida Keys. Here the narrow Overseas Highway hops and skips across a fragile chain of tiny, jewel-like islands, offering visitors a wealth of diversions, including a chance to visit Florida's spectacular coral reef, swim with dolphins, see miniature Key deer, and visit a unique museum dedicated to the history of diving. Eventually the road ends in the charming and slightly offbeat world of Key West. Here, elegantly rebuilt historic cottages line quiet streets, while blocks away, Duval Street offers an exciting world of shopping, dining, and the pulsing nightlife of legendary watering holes such as Hog's Breath Saloon and Sloppy Joe's Bar. What makes Key West special, though, is its vibrant culture, which comes from the people who call this island home. Here you will find a heady mix of original Cuban pioneers, the 1960s radicals who founded the Conch Republic, a newer wave of affluent get-away-from-it-all techsters, a thriving LGBT population, and generations of writers and other artists lured here, perhaps, by the ghost of "Papa" Hemingway.

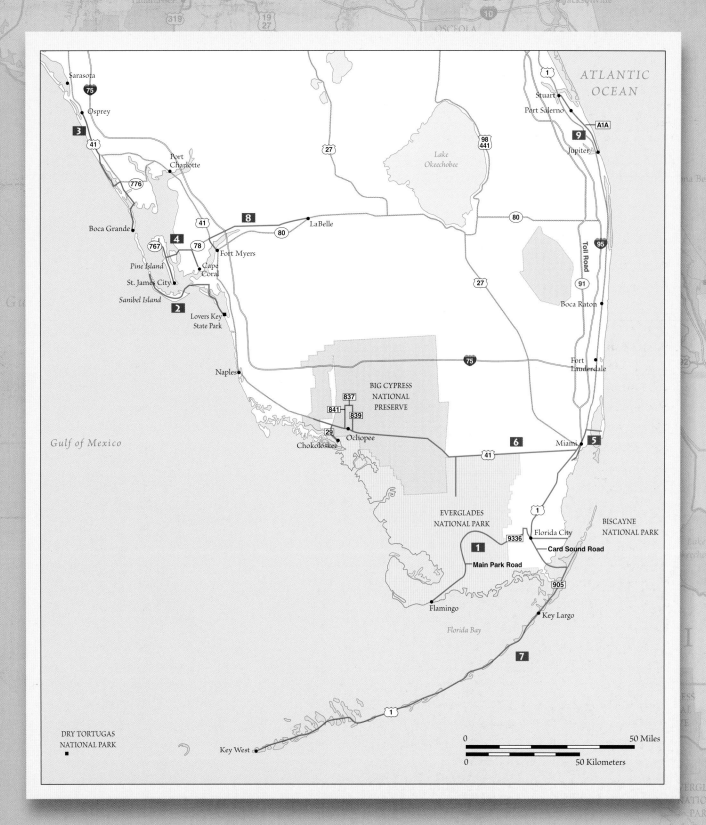

ATLANTIC OCEAN

Sarasota

Osprey

Port Charlotte

Boca Grande

Pine Island

St. James City

Sanibel Island

Lovers Key State Park

Naples

Gulf of Mexico

Fort Myers

Cape Coral

LaBelle

Lake Okeechobee

Boca Raton

Fort Lauderdale

Stuart

Port Salerno

Jupiter

Toll Road

BIG CYPRESS NATIONAL PRESERVE

Ochopee

Chokoloskee

EVERGLADES NATIONAL PARK

Miami

Florida City

Card Sound Road

Main Park Road

Flamingo

Florida Bay

Key Largo

BISCAYNE NATIONAL PARK

DRY TORTUGAS NATIONAL PARK

Key West

0        50 Miles

0        50 Kilometers

100 Miles

# 1

# MANGOES, MYSTERIES, and the RIVER of GRASS

## BISCAYNE NATIONAL PARK TO EVERGLADES NATIONAL PARK

*Begin in Biscayne National Park, and then drive west on SW 328th Street to SW 137th Avenue and turn north (right). Continue to SW 288th Street and turn south (left) until the junction with US Highway 1 N/S Dixie Highway/FL 5 and turn north (right) to Coral Castle, which is on the right just past the intersection with Biscayne Drive/SW 288th Street.*

*From Coral Castle, take Biscayne Drive west to SW 182nd Avenue (Robert's Drive) and turn north (right) to R. F. Orchids. Continue north on SW 182nd Avenue to SW 248th Street (Coconut Palm Drive), then turn west (left) to SW 187th Avenue (Redland Road) and turn south (left) to the Fruit and Spice Park. Return south along SW 187th Avenue (Redland Road) to SW 296th Street, and turn west (right) to SW 217th Avenue (Loveland Road) and then turn south (left) to Schnebly Redland's Winery. Continue south on SW 217th Avenue (Loveland Road) to SW 344th Street. There, turn east (left) to SW 192nd Avenue (Redland Road), where the Robert Is Here fruit stand is on the southeast corner. Continue south along SW 192nd Avenue (Redland Road) to State Route 9336, and turn south (right) to the entrance of Everglades National Park. After a stop at the visitor's center, follow the Main Park Road to Long Pine Key Road and turn left onto the Anhinga Trail. Return to the Main Park Road, and continue along it to Flamingo at the end of the road.*

Above: **A field in South Florida is watered by special trucks that draw water from shallow wells and spray it across the crops. The water table in much of South Florida is just below the surface of the ground.**

Opposite: **Two fishermen traverse a canal between Coot Bay and the Gulf of Mexico. This remote corner of the Everglades offers a tremendous variety of salt and freshwater fishing.**

South of Miami and above the Keys lies a vast plain of frost-free fertile land on which farmers grow crops that are cultivated in few other places in the continental United States: pineapples, mangoes, papayas, and giant, smooth-skinned avocados, not to mention ornamentals from exotic palm trees to rare orchids. Much of this land was once part of the Everglades, drained and converted to farmland during massive "flood prevention" projects between 1910 and 1950. Today, vast tracts of this farmland are being lost to what the farmers euphemistically call "the final crop"—housing developments spreading south from Miami. But around Homestead and Florida City, large tracts of lush farmland still lie undisturbed and are crisscrossed by small two-lane roads that invite travelers to glimpse some of old-time Florida.

Convoy Point in Biscayne National Park is a small but wonderfully relaxing seaside oasis and a great starting point for this journey. A few steps away, the visitor's center offers interesting displays that introduce you to the park's 172,000 acres, over 95 percent of which are underwater. Biscayne National Park's ecosystems include the shallow bay, the barrier islands, and the northernmost part of the world's third-largest barrier reef system, which begins here and extends almost two hundred miles along the Florida Keys to the Dry Tortugas. Most visitors who explore the park take one of the sightseeing tours. Snorkeling and scuba trips to the reef and sightseeing tours of Biscayne Bay are popular options. Guided canoe and kayak trips through the translucent waters of the bay are offered from late November through April.

Both Florida City and Homestead sport an amazing collection of small and intriguing attractions. One of the most famous Old Florida attractions is the curious and mysterious Coral Castle. What makes this massive structure unique is that the two-story tower and the giant, fanciful sculptures that fill the acre or so walled garden surrounding it were all carved by hand out of native coral rock by a ninety-five-pound Latvian immigrant named Edward Leedskalnin.

As the story goes, Leedskalnin was spurned by his sixteen-year-old fiancée and drifted around North America for several years. He ended up in the wilderness of south Florida around 1920 and, with little money or resources, spent the next twenty years building this monument to his lost love. Many mystics have speculated that Leedskalnin

A lipstick bush grows at the Fruit and Spice Park, a thirty-seven-acre botanical garden devoted to growing and displaying tropical fruits. The lipstick bush got its name for its colorful juice, which women in the nineteenth century used to make their lips red.

was able to harness spiritual powers to move the massive stones, while more technically minded investigators maintain that he was simply a masterful natural engineer gifted in understanding the power of leverage. Whatever his methods, his achievement is amazing. His creations include a nine-ton gate that once swung with the push of a single finger. Beyond the downtown areas, Homestead and Florida City abound with specialty tropical plant growers. One of the most interesting is R. F. Orchids, whose greenhouses produce tens of thousands of rare and beautiful orchids and bromeliads. Owner Robert Fuchs is a third-generation orchid grower and breeder renowned for his orchid tours to many exotic corners of the globe. Visitors to R. F. Orchids can tour the greenhouses and on weekends can even see Fuchs's fascinating private gardens next door.

Not far away, the unique Fruit and Spice Park offers

Exotic fruits, including guava, mangoes, papayas, carambola, and atamoya are for sale at the "Robert Is Here" fruit stand in Homestead. Owner Robert Moehling has been selling fruit on the same corner for almost fifty years.

thirty-seven acres of beautifully maintained grounds lushly planted with over 500 varieties of exotic fruit and spice trees, shrubs, and plants from around the world. There are 160 varieties of mango, 75 types of bananas, and 70 bamboo species on display. The park was established in 1942 as a county park dedicated to growing and displaying tropical fruits from around the world.

Inside the visitor's center, in the Mango Café, you can sample some of the exotic fruits grown here before you take one of the fascinating guided tours of the grounds.

Tucked near the edge of the Everglades, Schnebly Redland's Winery and Brewery specializes in award-winning wines made from the region's tropical fruits—mangoes, guavas, lychees, carambolas, and passionfruit. The brewery offers beers with citrus, coconut, and herb notes, and there is a farm-to-table restaurant. Tours and tastings are available, and on weekends, local musicians perform while visitors relax on the lawn in the outdoor grassy area bordered by lush tropical greenery.

If you prefer your exotic fruits *au naturel*, the place to stop is the Robert Is Here fruit stand on 344th Street in Homestead. "The name comes from when I was six years old," owner Robert Moehling said. "My dad put me on this corner with a bunch of cucumbers to sell. That first day I didn't sell any, so my dad figured we needed some marketing, so he painted a big sign that said: 'Robert Is Here!' The next day I sold all my cucumbers, and the rest is history!" For nearly fifty years, Robert has grown and sold exotic fruits—including mangoes, papayas, tamarinds, and strange-looking specimens with names like atemoya, carambola, and sapodilla—on this corner. His elaborate stand also offers jams, jellies, and, best of all, cool smoothies and shakes (the key-lime milkshake is legendary).

A few miles beyond Robert Is Here is the southern entrance to the Everglades. The visitor's center about a mile inside the park has excellent displays on the park and its wildlife. As you enter the park itself, you'll find that one of the first wildlife viewing areas is also one of the best in the park. The Anhinga Trail features paths and a boardwalk that winds through a wildlife-filled marsh. Here, you'll find a wealth of wading birds, including egrets, great blue and tricolored herons, and rare wood storks. You'll also have no trouble spotting alligators of all sizes lounging on the muddy banks or gliding in sinister silence through the dark waters. The park's main road continues southward, tracing a line through the vast panoramas and shallow waters of the "River of Grass," as writer Marjory Stoneman Douglas described the Everglades. Here, too, are stands of dwarf cypress and hardwood hammocks that are, in reality, islands in the river.

At the end of the road stands the tiny settlement of Flamingo. Once a thriving community on the edge of the great wetland, today Flamingo is mostly an administrative center for the park where you can launch your own boat; rent a kayak, canoe, powerboat, or houseboat; and take guided tours to explore the coastal mangrove mazes of Florida Bay. There is a store, gas station and seasonal (Thanksgiving–April) restaurant, gift shop and marina store. Still recovering from the devastation caused by Hurricane Wilma in 2005, the park service has approved a new, environmentally conscious hotel and a restaurant. In the meantime, this is a peaceful and lovely spot to sit and watch the wild world go by.

This is one of the few places in the United States where you can spot an American crocodile, and the only place where crocodiles (who like salt water) and alligators (who prefer fresh water) mingle. And at low tide, you can sit on the seawall and watch hundreds of white pelicans and other wading birds feed on the mud flats and roost in the surrounding mangroves of nearby islands, just as the fishermen who lived here in the 1930s may have done so long ago.

---

## 2

# SAND and SEASHELLS

## FORT MYERS BEACH TO CAPTIVA ISLAND

*Begin at Lovers Key State Park in Fort Myers Beach and drive northwest (left) on Estero Boulevard, and then turn north (right) onto San Carlos Boulevard and State Route 865. Continue to Summerlin Road and turn west (left). At McGregor Boulevard, turn southwest (left) and take Causeway Boulevard (a toll road) onto Sanibel Island. At the intersection with Periwinkle Way, turn east (left) to visit Lighthouse Point and the beach there. Return on Periwinkle Way through town and take a slight turn to the right onto Palm Ridge Road, which becomes Sanibel-Captiva Road. Turn right into J. N. "Ding" Darling National Wildlife Refuge. Continue on Sanibel-Captiva Road and turn left onto Bowman's Beach Road. Return to Sanibel-Captiva Road and continue on to Captiva Island, where the road name changes to Captiva Drive. Continue to Chapin Lane and turn left to the Chapel-By-The-Sea. Return to Captiva Drive and continue into the small village.*

Back in the day (to borrow an old-timers' phrase), Fort Myers couples seeking privacy would row their skiffs out to the beaches of the four small islands offshore to spend the day picnicking, swimming, and "spooning" (borrowing another old-timers' phrase). That's the reason these barrier islands, now linked to the mainland by a causeway, are known as Lovers Key. Lovers still come here, but so do families and anyone who wants to stroll along the outer islands' miles of pristine, shell-strewn beach.

Originally slated for development, these islands were saved from "Death by Condominium" at the eleventh hour by the state of Florida. Development of the area has been a key issue since the arrival of the first Europeans; not surprisingly, the locals have sometimes objected. It was not far from here, on Mound Key, that Ponce de Leon arrived at the end of his first voyage in 1513 and encountered the native Calusa people and their highly developed society. He returned here in 1521 to found a colony. The Calusa were not too keen on this idea, and during a skirmish, Ponce was struck in the thigh by an arrow. His wound festered and eventually killed him, although he made it back to Cuba before he died.

Above: **Sandpipers gather in the shallows of Bungee Beach near Sanibel Island in South Florida.**

Opposite: **Sea shells of many types lie scattered on the beaches of Sanibel Island. Sanibel is considered one of the best shelling spots in the Western Hemisphere.**

For years thereafter, Europeans pretty much lost interest in the area, and much of it lay wild and unvisited. It was so isolated that according to legend, when a pirate named Black Augustus was captured by the Spanish authorities, he managed to escape and live out the rest of his days undisturbed on Lovers Key.

A few miles north of Lovers Key, the town of Fort Myers Beach offers seven miles of broad, sandy beaches. Lynn Hall Memorial Park is a popular place to swim, relax, and enjoy the sun. Here, too, the five-hundred-foot-long Fort Myers Beach Pier is a great place to watch people on the beach, parasailers in the sky, families fishing from the pier, and spectacular sunsets over the Gulf of Mexico. Next door, bustling Times Square offers a colorful profusion of shops, casual eateries, and street performers.

Right: Colorful shops and restaurants line the sandy lane that runs through the tiny village of Captiva on Captiva Island.

Below: Shell collectors come from all over the world to search for seashell treasures on the beaches of Sanibel Island. On any day, you can see dozens of people bent over in what is humorously called the "Sanibel Stoop" as they scan for colorful or rare shells.

This is about as busy as life gets in the village of Captiva on Captiva Island.

A few miles further on, the long causeway to Sanibel Island offers splendid views of beautiful San Carlos Bay and the surrounding islands as you cross its two-mile length. If Lovers Key is pristine, Sanibel is refined yet friendly. People on this tidy and lovely island almost always have a ready smile. Maybe it's the fact that more than two-thirds of their island is protected from development by public parks, beaches, and the spectacular J. N. "Ding" Darling National Wildlife Refuge. The island is also home to wonderful bike paths that trace its length.

Best known for their fabulous abundance of seashells, Sanibel's beaches are popular places to be early in the morning, particularly after a night of storms and at low tide. Then the shellers are out in force, practicing the famous "Sanibel Stoop" as they sort through an amazing variety of shells with names like *tulip, junonia, lightning whelk,* and *angel wing.* The best places for shelling on the island include Lighthouse Beach at the southern end of the island and lovely Bowman's Beach to the north.

You can learn more about shells than you ever dreamed possible at the small but wonderfully creative Bailey-Matthews National Shell Museum. Here, exhibits show the variety of shells found here and around the world, how they are formed, and the myriad uses to which man has put them. Among the most memorable items on display are the incredibly ornate shell-patterned valentine boxes made by islanders in various ports around the world for nineteenth-century sailors to buy for their sweethearts back home.

Across the street from the shell museum is the J. N. "Ding" Darling National Wildlife Refuge. Named for the famous Pulitzer Prize–winning political cartoonist and conservationist who fought for its protection, the 6,300-acre reserve is home to dolphins, manatees, and a wealth of bird life, including the stunning, pink-plumed roseate spoonbills. The first way to explore this preserve is to join the slow parade of cars and bicycles following the four-mile Wildlife Drive that passes along the shore of several mangrove wetlands. Here, pelicans, spoonbills, and many other birds wade and hunt for food. The second way to see the refuge is to take a boat tour on Tarpon Bay, where you can often spot pods of dolphins feeding and cavorting, as well as eagles, ospreys, and an occasional manatee or two.

From Ding Darling, the road continues northward, eventually running close to the beach and crossing a short causeway to Captiva Island. According to legend, the island got its name when the pirate Gasparilla used it as a hide-away for women prisoners being held for ransom (the male prisoners having all been killed). A more likely story is that it got its name after the Calusa Indians held Spanish sailors captive there. In any event, Captiva is smaller and narrower than Sanibel—part of the reason it is more quiet and reclusive. The island's three-block downtown is a pretty place to stroll around, if only to enjoy its unique, offbeat flavor.

In a quiet corner at the south end of town stands the charming little wood-framed Chapel-By-The-Sea. This simple church is more than a hundred years old, having been built as the island school in 1901. If you happen to arrive on Christmas Eve, this is the busiest place in this area as some six hundred locals arrive to fill the chapel and surrounding grounds for a candlelight service and carol sing.

On most other days, the chapel is a tranquil place, the quiet sounds of surf providing a natural music by which to contemplate life and the beauty of the world around, or to just enjoy watching the sun set in a crimson glow beyond the dunes.

Families, sunbathers, and yes, lovers, all enjoy strolling the sandy strands of Lovers Key State Park.

---

### 3

# The PIRATE COAST

## SPANISH POINT TO BOCA GRANDE

*Begin in Historic Spanish Point in Osprey, on the west side of US Highway 41. Drive south on Highway 41 to Florida State Route 776, and continue south to County Road 774/Manasota Beach Road in the town of Woodmere, then turn west (right). Follow Manasota Beach Road when it turns south and then west onto Manasota Key, and then turn south (left) on Manasota Key Road and follow it the length of the key. Farther on, the name changes to North Beach Road. A short distance farther on, turn left (northeast) on Beach Road to return to the mainland. Turn right (southeast) onto South McCall Road/State Route 776 for a short distance. Then turn south (right) onto Placida Road. Turn southwest (right) and cross Gasparilla Bridge/Boca Grande Causeway onto Gasparilla Island, and turn south (left) on Gasparilla Road. In Boca Grande, turn west (right) on Fifth Street to cut over to Gilcrest Avenue and turn south (left). Gilcrest Avenue becomes Gulf Boulevard as it continues south to the Boca Grande Lighthouse.*

Few places in Florida can claim a history as long and layered as the tiny peninsula called Spanish Point. In 1867, John Webb and his family arrived at Spanish Point from Utica, New York to start a citrus and sugar cane farm. They were successful and soon were producing cane syrup and packing their citrus to ship to market. As their fortunes grew, they built a resort for northern visitors who came by ship to relax beside the tropical beauty of Little Sarasota Bay. The Webbs originally chose this point of land because it was elevated and offered protection from storms. The elevation was not natural, however, but man-made. The point was home to large mounds built from the shells of innumerable seafood dinners and other trash cast off by a native civilization that had lived here for five thousand years. An extensive archaeological excavation in the twentieth century uncovered more than four hundred burial sites

(including, inexplicably, one interred alligator), as well as a wealth of artifacts.

Today, Spanish Point is a living history museum where you can tour several buildings from the Webb pioneer era, as well as some from the early twentieth century when the land was the estate of wealthy widow, Bertha Honoré Palmer. The most fascinating attraction here, however, is a low building that shelters part of the original archaeological excavation. Visitors can actually walk into an excavated trench into the mound, where behind glass walls are layers of accumulated shells and cast-offs that represent thousands of years of human habitation.

From Spanish Point, the road winds its way along Little Sarasota Bay to a tiny causeway that leads just a short distance to Manasota Key. This island is unique, as one resident noted, because it "looks and feels the way much of coastal Florida did back in the 1950s—just a few houses, nothing pretentious and no high rises." A narrow two-lane road traces most of the island's eleven-mile length, passing attractive but simple beach homes and winding in sinuous curves through sun-dappled green canopies of live oak. The island boasts no museums or attractions and offers little to draw casual tourists other than ten or so miles of relaxing scenery. Manasota Key is also home to several fine beaches. The prettiest, by most counts, is the beach at Blind Pass Park. Here, the road follows the beach for half a mile, offering splendid views; and the seldom-crowded, shell-strewn strand is the perfect place to stroll, sunbathe, and forget the world at large.

Heading south from Manasota Key, the route follows Placida Road, which at one time connected several small fishing villages that once thrived along this shore. A short toll causeway connects Gasparilla Island and the town of Boca Grande to the mainland. The island is named for the swashbuckling pirate Gasparilla, who may be more of a myth than a real man. According to legend, Gasparilla was a dashing Spanish naval officer-turned-buccaneer who terrorized the Gulf Coast of Florida between 1783 and 1821, a period of almost forty years. During this time, Gasparilla, in proper pirate fashion, captured ships, killing the men but keeping the beautiful women as concubines on Captiva Island (hence its name).

Whether Gasparilla ever existed is open to debate, but what is true is that the drive down Gasparilla Island is

Fresh seafood is always for sale in the tiny town of Boca Grande on Gasparilla Island.

Top: The Victorian-era octagonal lighthouse on Boca Grande Island is a working light that has been guiding boats safely into Charlotte Harbor since it was built in 1890. A museum in the lighthouse covers island culture and history dating back twelve thousand years.

Lower left: Valencia oranges are prized for their sweet juice. The oranges are harvested in winter, but in early spring, the orchards are filled with the powerful fragrance of citrus blooms.

Lower right: Colorfully painted old-time gas pumps evoke nostalgia at this charming gift shop in Boca Grande.

lovely and serene. Toward the southern end of the island, a tall, steel tower lighthouse similar to the one on Sanibel can be seen rising high above the beach. This is not the historic Boca Grande Lighthouse, but a range-light used by mariners to line up with other lights as they navigate channels at night.

From here, it is just a short distance south to the real Boca Grande Lighthouse, an unusual, square Victorian structure with the light on the roof. The lighthouse was built in 1890 and manned until 1956, when it was automated. It was decommissioned in 1966 but recommissioned as a working light twenty years later after having been restored by a group of island citizens. Today, it is part of the state park system and contains a museum that relates the history of the island and the lighthouse. Surrounding the lighthouse on two sides is a stretch of beach that makes a charming spot to sit and watch small boats entering Charlotte Harbor or to pass the time with the locals who surf-cast from the rocks at the very end of the island.

From here, it's worth stopping for a few minutes to wander around the quaint little town of Boca Grande, browsing in the small boutiques or eating at one of the remarkably good restaurants that may or not be built on the very spot where Gasparilla buried his legendary treasure so long ago.

---

**4**

# PINE ISLAND SOJOURN

## CAPE CORAL TO ST. JAMES CITY

*Drive west on State Route 78/Pine Island Road west from Cape Coral, across the causeway and onto Little Pine Island and then continue to Pine Island. Turn north (right) on Stringfellow Road and take it to Pineland Road and turn west (left) into the town of Pineland. Pineland Road becomes Waterfront Drive, and then turn east (right) onto Caloosa Drive. Turn north (left) onto Robert Road, and then north (left) onto Stringfellow Road and continue north into Bokeelia and the end of the road. Turn around and take Stringfellow Road to the south end of the island and St. James City.*

Lacking fine, sandy beaches and the subsequent development that has occurred in so many places along this coast, Pine Island offers a fascinating glimpse of what the Florida Keys, or even the neighboring islands of Sanibel and Captiva, may have looked like decades ago. The island's wealth of mangrove shallows has, however, made it enormously popular with anglers, whose shallow-draft flat boats line the small canal communities at the northern and southern ends of the island. In between, long stretches of open road pass pretty palm and tropical plant nurseries, as well as some undeveloped expanses of native island forest.

Pine Island Road is the main route onto the island, and as it leaves the mainland it crosses through the funky roadside community of Matlacha (pronounced *mat-la-CHAY*). Barely a wide spot along the causeway, Matlacha is a fun place to park and stroll. Art galleries, restaurants, and small hotels stand shoulder-to-shoulder along the road, and it seems as if there's a contest to determine who can paint their establishment with the brightest colors. Although some of the shops look a bit rustic, inside you'll find quality paintings, glasswork, and sculptures by local as well as national artists. Behind the shops are small marinas and tiny trailer parks (where some of the trailers contain even more galleries) nestled along the fish- and wildlife-rich waters of Matlacha Pass.

The road crosses Little Pine Island, which is now a more pristine wetland than it was just a few years ago. When development in the Fort Myers area exploded in the 1960s, ditches were dug across Little Pine Island to drain the fresh water and relieve the number of mosquitoes here. Unfortunately, this action allowed invasive plants such as the Australian pine, melaleuca, and Brazilian pepper to flourish, destroying much of the traditional wetland habitat. In an unusual experimental program that began

Above: **A field of bougainvillea adds a brilliant splash of color to the landscape of rural Pine Island. The island is home to many growers of tropical landscape plants.**

Right: **A group of hand-painted mailboxes decorate a lane on Pine Island. The island has become a favorite place for artists and craftspeople to live.**

Opposite: **This narrow road leads to Bokeelia at the northern end of Pine Island. The small community is a quiet, out-of-the-way place favored by vacationers, retirees, and fishermen.**

in 1996, a developer contracted with the state of Florida to restore Little Pine Island's natural habitat in order to offset habitat loss in developments elsewhere. Planned and supervised by environmental scientists, this program has been a tremendous success. Today Little Pine Island is fully rejuvenated and is part of Charlotte Harbor Preserve State Park. Birds and wildlife are flourishing, with osprey, red-shouldered hawks, and rare wood storks claiming the island as their home.

Pine Island was home to a thriving Calusa culture long before the arrival of the first Europeans. Here, they built complex villages along canals and created huge shell mounds that were the high-end real estate of their day, offering safe haven during storms that flooded lower lands. The Calusa once dominated an area from Punta Gorda south to the Ten Thousand Islands.

*Sunrise at Pineland* by Merald Clark depicts the town chief at the Calusa village of Tampa (present-day Pineland).
*Courtesy of the Florida Museum of Natural History*

## THE CALUSA

When Ponce de Leon first encountered the Calusa in 1513, they numbered between twenty and fifty thousand, and they and their ancestors had lived along the southwest coast of Florida for thousands of years. They had a highly developed culture and dominated southern Florida, trading with and collecting tribute from other tribes as far away as modern-day Cape Canaveral.

Their government was centralized, and they undertook large-scale construction programs, such as building long canals to improve transportation and creating the 125-acre manmade island of Mound Key, which became their ceremonial center and capital. Also known as the Shell Indians, the Calusa planted some crops, but relied more on fishing, using sophisticated nets and traps. As warriors, they were fearless and known to board and attack the vessels of early European explorers. They were also skilled seamen, paddling ocean-going log canoes as far as Cuba.

The Calusa's downfall began with the first arrival of Europeans, who carried diseases such as smallpox, for which the Calusa had no natural resistance. The Calusa were devastated by these diseases, and as their strength ebbed, they were attacked by other native tribes from the north. Many were also captured and enslaved by the Spanish. However, in the end, they trusted the Spanish more than the British, and some reports suggest that the last Calusa retreated to Cuba when the Spanish ceded Florida to the British in 1763.

A great place to get an understanding of this fascinating native culture is near the north end of Pine Island in the village of Pineland. A historic marker by the waterfront notes that all of Pineland was once part of a shell-mound village. Much of the original shell mounds were used as road-building materials in the nineteenth and twentieth centuries, but at the nearby Randall Research Center you can see evidence of the sophisticated community that once stood here. The research center is an arm of the Florida Museum of Natural History, and the information center has displays about the Calusa and the archaeological work that has taken place here. Far more interesting is the two-thirds-mile-long Calusa Heritage Trail that winds among the actual excavations of a huge shell mound that once covered more than two hundred acres.

Pineland has no beaches to speak of, so when Pine Islanders want a hit of sun and sand, they hop in their boats and zip a few miles across Pine Island Sound to either Cayo Costa or North Captiva island. Both islands are accessible only by boat, and both have stretches of untouched beach reserved for public use as part of Cayo Costa State Park. In addition to privacy and undeveloped beauty, these sugar-white sand beaches offer some of the finest shell collecting in North America. Fortunately for boatless visitors, Tropic Star Cruises offers island shelling tours out of the Pineland Marina. A typical tour leaves at 9:30 in the morning and returns about 4:30, giving you a full day to enjoy shelling, beachcombing, picnicking, or simply relaxing along the island's nine miles of unspoiled sand and surf.

Stringfellow Road continues north through a landscape of exotic palm nurseries and tropical fruit and vegetable farms. Among the greenery that lines the road, you might spot plantings of mangoes, papayas, pineapples, and carambola (star fruit). The road ends at the little town of Bokeelia, which occupies the very northern tip of the island. There's little to do here other than shop at the elegant Crossed Palms Gallery, look at the pretty water, and drive through the resort, then turn around to work your way back. The

The colorful shops and galleries of Matlacha reflect the community's spirit of quirky independence. Located on the narrow strip of land that connects Pine Island and the mainland, the residents of Matlacha consider their little town "a world apart."

A group of chairs await vacationers in Bokeelia on Pine Island. The island's lack of fine sand beaches has helped ensure the relaxed atmosphere that artists, fishermen, and nature lovers enjoy.

road returns southward for eleven scenic miles to where the optimistically named small town of St. James City occupies the southernmost tip of the island. Here, you can park and walk to where the road ends at the water and look across the sound to nearby Sanibel Island. Once you've done that, a great way to end your island tour is to stop in the Waterfront Restaurant and try one of Florida's best grouper sandwiches, best enjoyed from a dockside table as the setting sun paints warm colors over the canals, boats, and palm trees. Ahhh . . . paradise!

---

## 5

# A RAMBLE THROUGH OLD MIAMI

### SOUTH BEACH TO COCONUT GROVE

*Begin at the Art Deco Welcome Center near the intersection of Ocean Drive and Tenth Street in Miami Beach. Head south along Ocean Drive to Fifth Street, and turn west (right) on Fifth Street, which becomes US Highway 41 N/FL A1A S/MacArthur Causeway W. Keep left to take Interstate 395 W toward Interstate 95/FL 836/Airport, and then merge onto Interstate 95 S via Exit 1A on the left. Take exit 1B toward US 41/SW 7th Street/Brickell Avenue and then merge onto NW Third Court and then west (right) onto SW Seventh St./US 41 S. Turn south (left) onto SW Sixteenth Avenue and then east (left) onto SW Eighth Street/US 41 N. The Little Havana Welcome Center is on the right just past SW Fifteenth Avenue.*

*Continue east on SW Eighth Street and turn south (right) onto SW Twelfth Avenue and then east (left) onto SW Twenty-Eighth Road. Immediately turn northeast (left) onto SW Ninth Avenue and then southeast (right) onto SW Twenty-Sixth Road. Just past Interstate 95, turn southwest (right) onto South Miami Avenue and then turn left into Vizcaya Museum and Gardens.*

*Turn southwest (left) onto S Miami Avenue, which becomes S Bayshore Drive, and then turn north (right) onto SW Seventeenth Avenue to S Dixie Highway/US Highway 1/FL 5. Turn southwest (left) and continue to Bird Road and make a slight right turn. Turn north (right) at Granada Boulevard, and in the roundabout take the second exit onto De Soto Boulevard to the Venetian Pool on your right.*

*Return southwest on De Soto Boulevard, and in the roundabout take the fourth exit onto Granada Boulevard back to Bird Road and turn east (left). Continue on Bird Road and then turn south (right) onto S Le Jeune Road/FL 953. In the roundabout, take the second exit onto Old Cutler Road and continue for two miles to Fairchild Tropical Botanic Garden on the left.*

*Return northeast on Old Cutler Road into the roundabout, and take the second exit onto FL 953. Almost immediately, turn east (right) onto Ingraham Terrace, which becomes Ingraham Highway as the road curves northeast, and then becomes S Douglas Road. Continue to the Kampong on the right.*

No place tells the story of Florida's coming-of-age better than bustling, urban Miami. Yes, we know there are no backroads to speak of here, but what the city does offer is a handful of very special places—some beautiful, some historic, some a bit quirky—that do an amazing job of communicating the sunshine state's vibrant history.

The place to start is South Beach, the wide, sun-dazzled strip of sand gracing the southernmost tip of the barrier island that protects Miami proper. A melting pot of the moneyed, fashionable, beautiful, and ultra-chic, South Beach is the glittering epicenter of the newest and trendiest of just about everything on the planet. Grab a cup of coffee at News Cafe overlooking the strand and just sit and watch the people go by. The crowd teems with well-tanned and muscled bodies, bikinied rollerbladers and dreadlocked dog-walkers. Fashion shoots happen almost daily along this strip, and models, photographers and the fashion-famous are common sights, along with lots of nattily dressed businessmen and the occasional well-known actor or musician strolling by.

Back in the heyday of the 1920s, Miami Beach saw its first wave of popularity as trains brought the affluent

Left: **The magnificent Vizcaya estate was built in the early twentieth century by tractor magnate James Deering. Today the house is operated as a museum that contains artwork and fine furnishings collected by Deering during his world travels. The gracious Italianate-style mansion is set on ten acres of lush formal gardens.**

Top right: **Miami's legendary South Beach is known for sun, sand, beautiful bodies, and the wild, funky—and sometimes just odd—architecture of its lifeguard stations. Every station is unique, and they have become beloved symbols of this world-famous strand.**

Bottom right: **A classic car adds a historic touch of class to the front door of one of South Beach's Art Deco hotels.**

travelers from the frosty North to the winter warmth of this beach. Classic and famous Art Deco hotels rose along Ocean Boulevard. South Beach has wisely helped to preserve many of these famous old establishments, including the Colony (#736), the Breakwater (#940), the Carlyle (#1250), and the Avalon (#700). The best time to appreciate them is at dusk, when the neon lights come on and it is easy to believe you have stepped back almost a century in time. Some of the hotels help this old-time feeling along by parking antique cars in front of the entrance.

The beach here is beautiful, fine white sand caressed by tropical blue waves. The Art Deco theme offers a taste of yesterday here as well, as the city has preserved its famously quirky and colorful lifeguard stations, some of

Above: **Neon lights and Art Deco hotels evoke the flavor of 1920s Miami in the midst of the glamour and glitz of trendy South Beach.**

Right: **If there is a spiritual heart to Little Havana, it is Máximo Gómez Park, also known as Domino Park on Calle Ocho, the "Main Street" of the community. Here people, mostly elderly Cuban men, play dominoes with lightning-fast moves and swap the news of the day.**

which are clearly Art Deco inspired, while others are just highly imaginative. South Beach is made for exploration on foot and the best place to start is at the Art Deco Welcome Center at 1001 Ocean Drive. The center offers daily guided walking tours of the Art Deco district (10:15 a.m.), as well as maps for self-guided walking tours and a museum that highlights the stunning architecture of 1920s–1930s Miami. Just a hundred yards from the welcome center you can gaze at the decidedly *not* Art Deco Villa Casa Casuarina, also known as the Versace Mansion. This elaborate Italianate manse was built by Alan Freeman, heir to the Standard Oil fortune, in 1930. It was at the front gate of this home that famed Italian designer Gianni Versace was murdered in 1997. Today, it operates as an exclusive boutique hotel.

After architecture and beautiful beaches, South Beach is best known for its nightlife. From sundown to the wee hours, the pulsing beat of dozens of nightspots attracts an international potpourri of beautiful people who come to dance and mingle the night away. The beach's vibrant LGBT culture adds to the lively night scene.

Just eight miles away by road, but a century away from South Beach in temperament, the beat and culture of Old Cuba thrives in Little Havana. The big attraction in

Little Havana is the absence of big attractions. It is a real neighborhood founded by those who have escaped communist Cuba over the past six decades. Calle Ocho is lined with their local businesses, and the sidewalk is dotted with Hollywood Boulevard–style pink stars that commemorate famous Latin musicians, actors, and personalities.

The best way to savor the cultural flavor of this neighborhood is to park and stroll along Calle Ocho (Eighth Street). Stop by to watch the residents play dominoes in Máximo Gómez Park (better known as Domino Park). The park is decorated in a domino theme and features tables where the players, mostly older gentlemen but also some women, sip Cuban coffee and sit in studied concentration.

If the delicious aroma of Cuban coffee tempts you, the best place to sample this delight is at El Pub, a family-owned restaurant where the decor is 1950s Cuba and the coffee is hot, smooth, and sweet. Other worthwhile Little Havana stops include Tower Theater, which has shown Spanish-English films and other international fare for decades; the Cuban Tobacco Cigar Company, where you can watch cigars being made by hand; and Los Pinareños Frutería, a traditional Cuban-style fruit and vegetable stand, where you can get fresh-made smoothies and other delicious snacks.

Before the roaring 1920s brought a vast real estate boom and bust to South Florida, wealthy families had discovered Miami and were buying up land and building great estates. One of these high-society pioneers was James Deering, who made his fortune as one of the principals of International Harvester, the farm equipment manufacturer. Deering traveled through Europe, and particularly Italy, studying the architecture and collecting paintings, sculpture, and furnishings to decorate the home he envisioned. It took him twelve years, from 1910 to 1922, to build his grand, bay-front Italianate-style estate, which he called Vizcaya.

Today this remarkable mansion—a reminder of Miami's first and all-too-brief gilded age—is open to the public as a museum. The estate features thirty-four period-decorated rooms, and over twenty-five hundred works of art. Surrounding the estate are ten acres of lush formal gardens that include a collection of over two thousand varieties of orchids.

The 1920s brought plenty of growth to South Florida, and one of the most successful developments was Coral Gables, just south of Miami. Here, elegant Mediterranean-style homes were built for wealthy and upper-middle-class buyers, often refugees from the cold northern states. The homes were built from native limestone, called *coral rock*, mined in a nearby quarry. As part of the development, the quarry itself was flooded to create a giant swimming pool that served as a backdrop to a glamorous casino. In the evenings, well-dressed residents gambled in the casino and dined around the luxurious pool, which was lavishly decorated with topical plantings, an arched bridge, elegant statuary, and tile-roofed buildings, in an attempt to evoke the romance of Venice, Italy. At times, the entire 820,000-gallon pool was drained so that the Miami Symphony Orchestra could perform on the floor, taking advantage of the quarry's amazing natural acoustics. The Venetian

A water lily graces a pool at the Kampong, the home that David Fairchild built beside Biscayne Bay. Sometimes called the "Indiana Jones" of exotic plant collectors, Fairchild traveled the world collecting rare, unusual, and often very useful tropical plants, which he brought back to Florida to propagate.

Casino eventually closed, but the Venetian Pool has remained a popular destination. If you bring a towel and a bathing suit, for a modest fee you, too, can dive into the azure waters, lazily paddle below the jungle-adorned waterfall, and imagine that you are *Tarzan* star Johnny Weismuller swimming here in the early days.

If you have ever eaten a pistachio or nectarine grown in this country, you have David Fairchild to thank for it. Those two species are among the twenty thousand or more plants that Fairchild collected from around the world and brought back to America. Fairchild, just one of the many fascinating people that settled in the Miami area in the 1920s, was instrumental in founding Fairchild Tropical Botanic Gardens in Cape Coral, a few miles south of the Venetian Pool. Here, on eighty-three acres you can wander to your heart's content along paths that lead through shady stands of flowering trees, beside lakes, and to gardens that represent tropical environments from around the globe.

Many of the plants are specimens that Fairchild collected on his world adventures.

But you can get a more personal view of this remarkable scientist and traveler by visiting his nearby home, which he called the Kampong (admission is by request but is usually accommodated, even on short notice). Here, on eight acres fronting Biscayne Bay, Fairchild built a lovely Asian-style home and cultivated hundreds of the tropical plants he collected. Today, it is the only part of the National Tropical Botanic Gardens in the continental United States (other parts are in the Hawaiian Islands). Stroll through the gardens and then walk down to the bay, where a lone bright red bench shaded by palms beckons. Here it is easy to imagine that you are one of Miami's founding elite, enjoying the tranquil and tropical beauty of your own estate, in the days when Miami was young and the future held the promise of pleasure and wealth.

## 6

# The TAMIAMI TRAIL

### MIAMI TO CHOKOLOSKEE

*From Miami, take US Highway 41, the Tamiami Trail, west to the Shark Valley Loop Road, turn south (left) and enter Everglades National Park. Return to US Highway 41 and continue west. Beyond Ochopee, turn north (right) on the unpaved Birdon Road and continue along Birdon to Wagon Wheel. There, turn east (right) and go to Turner River Road. From there, turn south (right) and return to US Highway 41. Turn west (right) and continue past Ochopee and State Route 29 to the Marsh Trail on the south side of US Highway 41. Return east to State Route 29 and turn south (right) to Everglades City. Continue south on Route 29, which becomes Copeland Avenue and then Smallwood Drive, to Chokoloskee.*

It may look like just another pretty two-lane Florida byway, but it took hundreds of laborers, three million sticks of dynamite, and thirteen years of backbreaking effort to build the first road to span the Everglades. Begun in 1915, the effort to link Tampa and Miami with a road through the then-impenetrable wetlands of Florida's interior required developing unique construction techniques specifically for the Everglades. The challenge was complex—after all, how do you build a road across a ten-inch-deep sheet of water flowing over a solid layer of limestone?

First, crews with machetes cleared the underbrush; then they laid a primitive set of rails so that a massive drilling machine could move forward. The drilling machine bored large holes in the limestone, and dynamite was packed in the holes. After it was detonated, custom-built steam shovels scooped the broken bedrock up to create a ditch, then the rock was placed next to the ditch to form the roadbed. In its early days, driving the Tamiami Trail was a novelty in itself, and it wasn't long before colorful and tacky tourist traps sprang up all along its length. Alligator

Birdon Road leads into the wilds of Big Cypress National Preserve, one of the best bird- and wildlife-watching areas in South Florida.

wrestling, airboat rides, and reptile zoos were all popular. The zoos and the wrestlers are mostly gone today, but the airboat rides continue to be popular and are a great way to experience the 'glades close up.

Located about fifteen miles west of Krome Avenue, the Everglades Safari Park offers traditional airboat rides. Driven by airplane propellers (and very loud engines), airboats glide almost frictionless along the water's surface, reaching speeds up to forty-five miles per hour. A typical ride lasts about an hour, during which you will almost certainly see alligators and numerous birds in their natural habitat. After the ride, the park presents an excellent twenty-minute educational program on alligators and other crocodilians, featuring a trainer working with live (and large) 'gators. After the show, you are welcome to stroll around the wetland enclosures where one or more of almost every type

Right: An airboat takes visitors for a ride into the Everglades. Airboats offer an exhilarating way for people to explore the watery wilderness of Florida's largest national park.

Below: Smallwood's General Store today looks much as it did in 1910, when it was the social center of this tiny community at the edge of the Everglades.

Big Cypress National Preserve offers a chance to observe rare and colorful birds like this tri-colored heron that is silently watching the water and waiting for his dinner to arrive.

of crocodilian on earth dwells. If you are lucky, Monster, an aptly named sixteen-foot alligator, will make an appearance, lumbering out of the airboat canal to sunbathe nonchalantly on the bank a few yards from a park walkway.

A few miles farther along the Tamiami Trail, a well-marked turn leads into the Everglades National Park Shark Valley Visitor's Center. This center is the starting point for a fourteen-mile round-trip tram tour of the Everglades. Narrated by a knowledgeable guide, the tram tour travels at a stately seven miles-per-hour down a narrow park road into the heart of the Everglades. Alligators can be seen in several places along the tour, and egrets, herons, and other wetland birds also are common here. The highlight of the tour is arriving at the three-story-high observation tower that allows a panoramic view of the seemingly limitless plain of golden sawgrass and hardwood hammocks that

make up the Everglades. The unpaved road to the observation tower is also open to hikers and bikers, and either of these methods can allow you to travel at your own pace in order to bird- and alligator-watch to your heart's content.

Continuing west along the Tamiami Trail, the landscape slowly changes from sawgrass plains to forest as you enter the Big Cypress National Preserve. The preserve was created to protect the Big Cypress region from development and allow the native Seminole and Miccosukee bands, who had called Big Cypress home for over a hundred years, to continue to live here and use the land. Much of the roadway here is bordered by cypress stands, where egrets, herons, and waterfowl are a common sight. Two points of interest along this stretch are worth investigating. The first is Clyde Butcher's Gallery. A renowned photographer and environmentalist, Butcher has been carrying his

## RESTORING NATURE ON A GRAND SCALE

In 1934, the federal government set aside 1.3 million acres of wetlands in southern Florida and created the Everglades National Park. The effort was spearheaded by a land developer-turned-conservationist named Ernest Coe. He had become alarmed at the rate that development and agriculture were swallowing up Florida's unique wilderness.

In 1947, the year the park officially opened to the public, Marjory Stoneman Douglas published her landmark book, *Everglades: The River of Grass*, which took the first hard look at the fragile and intertwined ecosystems of these wetlands and the damage that was being done by the encroachment of developments and construction projects such the Tamiami Trail, which created a dam across the Everglades, blocking the slow-flowing sheet of water that was the Everglade's lifeblood. Moreover, severe floods in the 1920s and 1930s prompted the creation of what grew to be 1,000 miles of levees and 720 miles of canals that directed vital water away from the Everglades and into the Atlantic. The result was catastrophic. By some accounts as much as 90 percent of the bird and wildlife have vanished from the region, and the lack of freshwater flowing into Florida Bay (along with dramatic increases in fertilizer and other pollutants contributed by agriculture and suburbs bordering the park) has created an annual occurrence of dead zones, where oxygen depletion kills sea grasses, fish, and all marine life for hundreds of square miles.

In 2000, the government, working in concert with farmers, city planners, and environmental groups, created the ambitious thirty-year, $7.8 billion Comprehensive Everglades Restoration Plan (CERP) to restore the Everglades. Central to the plan is the need to restore as much of the original flow of water through the 'glades as possible by filling in canals that send water to the Atlantic, storing water in vast underground chambers for use during droughts, and raising long sections of the Tamiami Trail and Interstate 75 on bridge-like "skyways" that allow free flow of water underneath.

An early portion of the project involved restoration of the Kissimmee River. The Army Corps of Engineers rerouted the river into a canal in the 1970s, but the canal is now being backfilled and the river is being returned to its original serpentine route, allowing the slower-flowing water to arrive cleaner at Lake Okeechobee. As of 2015, in spite of funding delays and planning challenges due to everything from invasive species to climate change, numerous major water handling and storage projects throughout South Florida have broken ground, giving hope to the vision of a thriving and healthy Everglades by midcentury.

An American alligator at Anhinga Overlook in Everglades National Park

Above: **A boardwalk offers a unique view of a cypress swamp in Big Cypress National Preserve. The preserve protects 729,000 acres of wetlands and unique ecosystems.**

Right: **The smallest post office in the United States is found in Ochopee, Florida. The tiny building was once just a service shed, but when the original post office burned down, it became the town's official post office.**

large-format camera into the Everglades (and wild places throughout the United States) for many years to record the wilderness he loves. His photography has been compared to that of the great Ansel Adams, and his showroom offers spectacular large-format prints of his photos and copies of his many books.

The other stop of interest is the Ochopee Post Office. This tiny wood-frame shack measures just eight feet four inches by seven feet three inches, making it officially the smallest post office in the United States. The post office was originally in the Ochopee General Store, which stood on this site until it burned down. The current building was just a pipe shed, but, necessity being the mother of architecture, the shed was moved closer to the road and pressed into service as the new post office.

One of the best ways to enjoy the natural beauty of Big Cypress while doing some bird-watching in the process is to follow the long loop of well-maintained gravel roads that lead into the reserve's interior north of Ochopee. The loop is formed by Turner, Upper Wagonwheel, and Birdon Roads. Traveling the length of Turner River Road is particularly scenic, where the canal along the road backs against an old cypress forest and the wetland and trees are alive with wildlife. Alligators glide silently along the mirror-like waters, and herons, egrets, and wood storks stalk the shore and rest in tree branches. If you don't take binoculars with you, you may find yourself jealously eyeing those carried by the many nature watchers who stop along the road to view this wealth of wildlife.

Back on the Tamiami Trail, head west for about sixteen miles to the Ten Thousand Islands National Wildlife Refuge, where a short hiking trail leads to an observation tower that offers wonderful views across the wildlife-filled wetlands. The Ten Thousand Islands is a maze of mangrove islands and inlets that extends around the southern end of Florida from the Everglades National Park to the Florida Keys. Teeming with wildlife and birds, this area is popular with anglers, naturalists, and anyone who loves the tropical outdoors— especially kayakers and canoeists, who can paddle the ninety-nine-mile-long Wilderness Waterway Trail.

Returning east on the Tamiami Trail, turn south along State Route 29, following it to the steamy town of Everglades City. This is the best place to find a restaurant or hotel or to take a guided paddling tour of the Ten Thousand

Islands. Everglades City is also home to the Museum of the Everglades, which offers historic photos and displays that relate the human history of the Everglades and the creation of Everglades City and Everglades National Park.

The road continues a few more miles through an amazing landscape of wetlands and mangrove islands to Chokoloskee. This tiny community has existed since about 1870, when the original settlers worked as hunters, farmers, and fishermen and supplemented their income by plume-hunting, making cane syrup, and making charcoal. One of the settlement's two merchants was Ted Smallwood; today his waterfront supply store still stands high above the water on stilts and is operated as a museum. Inside, the shelves are lined with patent medicines, soaps, fabrics, and general supplies, just as they would have been when the store was in full operation around 1910. Outside, you can sit on a picnic bench and enjoy watching the parade of boats that passes by as fishermen head out to try their luck in the vast mangrove wilderness that has changed little since Ted Smallwood sold supplies here one hundred years ago.

---

## 7

# The FLORIDA KEYS

### MIAMI TO KEY WEST

*Head south out of Miami on US Highway 1 to Florida City. Bear left (south) on Card Sound Road to Key Largo, where the road is also known as County Road 905A. Turn right (southwest) on County Road 905, which reconnects with US Highway 1, the Overseas Highway. All destinations along the Overseas Highway have a mile marker reference number.*

Although calling the Overseas Highway a backroad is a bit of a misnomer, it is undeniably one of the most spectacular highways in America. Following the route of Henry Flagler's original Overseas Railroad, the road connects a string of islands with forty-four long bridges. Where it crosses islands, it presents a mix of Florida kitsch, elegant resorts, trailer parks inhabited by millionaires, and a surprising number of green spaces and wetlands that the residents have jealously protected from the voracious forces of development.

Beyond the road lies a different world altogether. To a pilot flying a thousand feet above, the road appears as a tiny thread of civilization tracing a line through a limitless

liquid world scattered with dazzling emerald islands. To the north lies the watery, mangrove wilderness of Florida Bay, a wildlife-filled estuary that lies between the outermost Keys and the Everglades. To the south, the great Florida Reef follows the scimitar-like curve of the Keys from Biscayne Bay to the Dry Tortugas, seventy miles beyond Key West. It is this colorful tropical wilderness of land and sea that have made the Keys a magnet for naturalists, bird-watchers, divers, snorkelers, fishermen, kayakers, canoeists, and boaters of all kinds.

To reach the Keys, most people simply drive south on Highway 1, but a better way is to follow the smaller Card

Sound Road across the broad wetland of Card Sound, passing rag-tag houseboat communities that are a reminder of the Keys of yesteryear. This road ends at the northern end of Key Largo, much of which—except for the four-thousand-acre ultra-posh Ocean Reef Club Resort at the tip—is preserved by the large Crocodile Lake National Wildlife Refuge (not open to the public). True to its name, the reserve protects breeding grounds of the endangered American crocodile, while keeping this end of the island pleasantly undeveloped.

Key Largo was immortalized in the Humphrey Bogart movie of the same name, and although he spent little time here (most of the movie was filmed on the Warner lot), Key Largo-ites still consider the island Bogey's spiritual home. Some scenes of the movie were filmed at the nearby Caribbean Club, and the club walls are covered with photos and other memorabilia. But the biggest souvenir from the island's Bogey era is found at the Holiday Inn

Right: **Two colorfully dressed women share a laugh outside their shop near Pigeon Key, Florida.**

Below: **Duval Street is much tamer now than it was a decade ago. By day, it offers up a potpourri of shops, galleries, and restaurants. By night, it is still the go-to place for music and revelry, with old-time favorites like Sloppy Joe's Bar providing refreshments for the nightly parade of folks doing the "Duval Pub Crawl."**

## FLAGLER'S FOLLY

If Florida has a founding father, it might be entrepreneur and oilman Henry Flagler. Flagler had already made and lost a fortune in salt mining by the time a young upstart named John D. Rockefeller approached Flagler's wealthy father-in-law to ask for $100,000 to start an oil refinery. Rockefeller was told that he could have the money if he accepted young Henry Flagler as his partner. Together they founded what would become the colossal Standard Oil Company.

In 1881, Flagler traveled to Florida in search of healing warmth for his ailing wife. While there, he quickly grasped that the warm climate, if combined with fine hotels and amenities, could attract hordes of winter visitors. What was needed, though, was a

**Detail from a column at the Ponce de Leon Hotel in St. Augustine.**
*Courtesy of the Library of Congress*

(mile marker 100), where the original *African Queen*—the boat from the Bogart-Hepburn classic—is on display and will take paying visitors for a ride.

Calling itself the Diving Capital of the World, Key Largo is the closest access point to the spectacular coral reef that runs the length of the Keys. Home to more than fifty species of coral and five hundred species of fish, the reef is protected as part of the John Pennekamp Coral Reef State Park and the Florida Keys National Marine Sanctuary. John Pennekamp Coral Reef State Park (mile marker 102.5) offers daily snorkeling, glass-bottom boat, and diving tours. Snorkeling tours last two-and-one-half hours and are geared to beginners. Once in the water, you swim along the reef where a myriad of colorful parrot fish, damselfish, spiny lobsters, and silvery sleek barracudas dart to and fro along the colorful coral ridge. You may also notice conchs lumbering along the sandy bottom. All but extinct in Florida a few years ago, these conchs are part of an intensive repopulation effort that began in 2006 and is showing great promise. Even if you don't visit the reef, there is plenty to do at John Pennekamp. Trails lead through the fascinating and lovely mangrove wetlands, and

bird-watchers will enjoy the many ibis, egrets, herons, and other birds that frequent the waterways.

Diving is also the focus of one of the Keys's newest and most fascinating attractions, the History of Diving Museum in Islamorada (mile marker 83). The museum is the passionate project of Dr. Joe Bauer and Dr. Sally Bauer, who traveled the world amassing the world's largest collection of historic dive gear, including dive helmets, armored suits, dive pumps, and accessories dating back to the 1600s. The museum uses the collection to relate the four-thousand-year history of diving. Various rooms are devoted to Florida treasure hunters, military diving, helium diving, the development of SCUBA, and modern-day pressurized armor suits used to dive to mind-boggling depths.

As you travel farther down the Keys, you may get the feeling that with every mile you are leaving America and the known world farther behind. This is not that surprising. After all, Key West did officially secede from America in 1982, declaring itself to be the independent Conch Republic. And while Key West was the official secessionist, the rest of the Keys were with it in spirit. The islands were protesting a new checkpoint that searched way to get them to Florida. Flagler started by building the superb 540-room Ponce de Leon Hotel in St. Augustine and buying the Jacksonville & Atlantic Railroad, which he renamed the Florida East Coast Railway.

His hotel was a great success, and Flagler soon began looking southward and dreaming of Florida's Atlantic Coast as an "American Riviera." He extended his railroad to Palm Beach and on to what was then the almost nonexistent settlement of Miami. Finally, he began dreaming of a railroad to Key West, where he envisioned creating both a tourism resort and what would become the closest American shipping port to the Panama Canal.

His critics (and more than one qualified engineer) thought he was daft, calling the idea of a railroad across the shallow waters of Florida Bay "Flagler's Folly." Flagler, however, had faith in the new science of building with reinforced concrete, and in 1905 an army of laborers and engineers began construction. The effort took over six years and cost what was—for the time—an unimaginable fortune of $27 million. Many laborers lost their lives to disease and in accidents, and more than 130 drowned during the 1906 Florida Keys Hurricane. But in 1912, eighty-three-year-old Flagler triumphantly rode his train into Key West. Many of Flagler's investments and the Florida tourism business thrived. The Key West railroad, however, never saw a profit, and in 1935 a Category 5 hurricane damaged it beyond repair. Ironically, a few years later "Flagler's Folly" came to life once more as the Overseas Highway, which was built on the foundations of the railway and ushered in the modern era of auto tourism to the Keys.

all vehicles returning from the Keys for drugs and illegal immigrants. The checkpoint, islanders argued, was hurting tourism, and when their pleas fell on deaf ears, Key West town council and Mayor Dennis Wardlow declared the island's independence.

Strictly tongue-in-cheek, the independence lasted exactly one minute, and then—borrowing the plot from the 1959 Peter Sellers movie *The Mouse That Roared*—Key West declared war on, and then quickly surrendered to, the United States, immediately requesting $1 billion in aid. While humorous, the protest also garnered international headlines, and the roadblock was removed. Today, the spirit of the Conch Republic is still alive and well, and the closer you get to Key West the more often you can spot Conch Republic flags, T-shirts, and bumper stickers.

Before you get to Key West, however, you may want to stop at the Dolphin Research Center (mile marker 59). The nonprofit center uses money raised from visitors and donations to fund studies that include testing dolphin

An eye-catching fishing and motel sign near Islamorada, Florida, glows as night begins to fall in the Keys.

Left: Bahia Honda State Park contains one of the Florida Keys' rare sandy beaches. In addition to the sun-drenched 2.5 mile-long stretch of sand, the park offers camping, hiking and biking trails, and a wide range of fishing and boating activities.

Center: A speedboat navigates one of hundreds of narrow channels in the Florida Keys.

intelligence, studying dolphin parenting, and developing better understanding of human/dolphin interaction. If you are in the mood to get wet with a marine mammal, this is a great place to do it. You can choose from a number of educational programs that include day-long encounters that let participants work alongside dolphin researchers and trainers and include in-the-water time with the dolphins.

Farther on, one of the few fine-sand beaches in the Keys can be enjoyed at Bahia Honda State Park. This park is a small gem and, after John Pennekamp Coral Reef State Park, is a great place to enjoy a snorkeling tour. Kayaking is also popular here; you can rent kayaks by the hour to explore the crystal-clear, fish-filled shallows that surround the island.

As you cross Big Pine Key, pay attention to the traffic signs asking you to slow as you are entering the realm of the endangered Key deer. These tiny relatives of white-tailed

deer stand barely thirty inches tall at the shoulder and weigh just fifty to seventy-five pounds. They have little fear of humans and can often be found grazing in backyards and along roadways.

Key West is really two islands. For many, it is Duval Street, where young and old gather to celebrate, people-watch, have a fun time, and stroll along this vibrant street that extends for more than a dozen blocks. This is Key West's shopping district, with souvenir and T-shirt shops, jewelry stores, boutiques, and art galleries. Legendary restaurants and bars abound, including Sloppy Joe's and the Bull and Whistle. After the sun goes down, the party atmosphere intensifies and you can join the Duval Crawl to visit the many bars and clubs to drink and dance the night away.

The other Key West is the old island—the one loved by legendary author Ernest Hemingway and inhabited by

Right: **Saltwater fly fishing is one of the most popular sports in the Florida Keys. Enthusiasts cast into very shallow water trying to attract tarpon, bonefish, permit, and other gamefish.**

descendants of the Bahamians and Cubans who settled here in the nineteenth century. This is the Key West of simple but elegant Conch homes with their shady porches and tin roofs. The best way to explore this world is by walking or renting a bicycle and pedaling along the quiet residential streets, perhaps stopping at a small restaurant for steaming café con leche and a hot, greasy, sinfully delicious Cuban sandwich.

Whichever Key West you have in mind, there are several things you'll want to do while you are here. One is to have breakfast under the tropical almond trees at Blue Heaven Restaurant. In decades past, the downstairs of this building hosted cockfights and boxing matches frequented by many, including "Papa" Hemingway. The upstairs housed a dance hall and bordello. Today, it serves the best banana pancakes you've ever tasted. Don't mind the chickens that wander around the tables—they're just part of the local color.

Another Key West must is a visit to Hemingway's house, the elegant home where he wrote *Death in the Afternoon*, *The Snows of Kilimanjaro*, and *For Whom the Bell Tolls*. Here, you can tour the house and his backyard studio and see the swimming pool that was the first in Key West. When it was built in the late 1930s, it cost an astounding $20,000 (more than $250,000 in today's dollars).

Not far from the Hemingway house stands the fascinating Mel Fisher Maritime Museum. Fisher was Florida's most renowned treasure hunter, whose famously optimistic slogan was "Today's the Day!" After many years of todays that weren't the day, Mel finally found the Nuestra Señora de Atocha, which sank in 1622 carrying a vast fortune in gold and silver. The museum has captivating displays of the treasure and first-class exhibits on the Atocha and other treasure ships that Fisher excavated. You can even

A tiny Key deer poses on a front lawn for a photo. Large portions of Big Pine Key are part of the National Key Deer Refuge, created to protect this rare and endangered species. The deer, which rarely get taller than thirty inches at the shoulder, can often be seen on the island, particularly on roadsides and in residents' yards near dusk.

purchase jewelry made from real coins that were on the ocean floor for almost four centuries.

Finally, everyone should visit the southernmost point of the United States, marked by a brightly painted buoy embedded in the sidewalk, to have your picture taken. Then walk or cab to Mallory Square for the sunset celebration, a carnival-like affair that attracts some of the country's wildest and most creative buskers. Regulars have included fire jugglers and a man who has trained housecats to do tricks, including leaping through a flaming hoop. If you like your entertainment a little less frantic, try a sunset sail aboard one of the schooners that operate from the nearby harbor. The trip usually includes buffet dinner served on deck and a chance to witness the legendary green flash that occurs in the last seconds as the sun passes below the watery horizon.

---

## 8

# The WILD CALOOSAHATCHEE RIVER

### FORT MYERS TO LABELLE

*Beginning at Edison Ford Winter Estates in Fort Myers, drive southwest on McGregor Boulevard/FL 867, and almost immediately turn southeast (left) onto Llewellyn Drive to Cleveland Avenue/US Highway 41N/FL 45. Then turn north (left) to cross the Caloosahatchee River into North Fort Myers. Turn east (right) at Pondella Road and then north (left) onto N Tamiami Trail/US 41 Business/FL 739. Turn east (right) onto Bayshore Road/FL 78. At the intersection with State Highway 31, turn north (left) to continue on FL 78/County Road 78, and after one mile watch for the junction with North River Road and turn east (right) to continue on FL 78 through the town of Alva. Continue along FL 78/County Road 78 as the road turns north, and then as the road turns east again, watch for Cemetery Road and, just past it, the turn for the Fort Denauld Bridge. Turn south (right) onto Fort Denauld Bridge Road/FL 78A Connector, and cross the Caloosahatchee River over the historic Swing Bridge. Continue south for a short distance, then turn east (left) onto Fort Denaud Road/FL 78A and then northeast (left) onto State Road 80 into LaBelle. Turn north (left) at Hardee Street and then left onto Fraser Avenue to the Captain Hendry House on the right.*

*Return east on Fraser Avenue to Main Street and turn north (left) for a block to Fort Thompson Avenue and turn east (right). Then turn north (left) onto Bridge Street/FL 29 and the Curtis Honey Company is on your right.*

*To return to Fort Myers, you can either continue north on Bridge Road, drive across the river, and then turn west (left) onto County Road 78. Or, drive south on Bridge Road to Hickpochee Avenue/State Road 80 and turn west (right).*

Palmetto trees frame a wild stretch of sandy beach at Lovers Key State Park, near Fort Meyers.

Left: In the early twentieth century, inventor Thomas Edison fell in love with the Fort Meyers area and built his winter home here. He also built a large laboratory that has been preserved as part of the Edison and Ford Winter Estate Museum.

Right: Thomas Edison enjoyed gardening in the warmth of Florida winters, and his winter estate was surrounded by lush tropical gardens, fountains, and landscaping.

In the late 1800s, much of southern Florida's interior looked more like the Wild West than a tropical paradise. This was a land of rough wilderness and rambling cattle ranches worked by wiry-tough Florida cowboys who proudly called themselves "crackers." Through the heart of this ranchland and wilderness wound the wild and mysterious Caloosahatchee River. The river was a highway into Florida's interior and had been since the Caloosa Indians paddled their canoes along its serpentine curves two thousand years ago. A few miles upstream from where the river emptied into Charlotte Harbor, the small dusty cow town of Fort Myers had risen up, with some three hundred hardy residents. It was into this town, in 1885, that a well-dressed man in his thirties stepped off a fishing boat he had hitched a ride on. He had escaped the cold of New Jersey that winter and travelled south to the refined resort town of St. Augustine only to find that they, too, were in the grip of a cold spell. So he headed by train and boat across Florida, then farther south, seeking warmth. At thirty-eight years of age, he was already world-famous and breathtakingly wealthy as a result of his remarkable inventions. His name was Thomas Edison.

Edison immediately took to the natural beauty and homespun hospitality of Fort Myers. So much so that, within days, he purchased a 13.5-acre parcel on the banks of the Caloosahatchee river. Several years later, Edison built his winter home here, along with a state-of-the-art laboratory that rivaled his famous one in Menlo Park. He and his family spent winters here; as the town's most famous resident, his arrival day and his birthdays became causes for parades and picnics.

Edison also attracted the rich and famous, who visited his estate frequently. One of these was a young Henry Ford, who had worked for Edison as a chief engineer at his electric plant in Detroit. After building his own version of an automobile, he established his own manufacturing plant, eventually developing revolutionary new ways to build cars more cheaply and efficiently. Edison had encouraged him constantly, and the two men had become fast friends. Like Edison, Ford enjoyed Fort Myers and eventually built his winter estate next to Edison's. Together, the two families camped and explored the natural beauty of Florida's southwest. In particular, they loved boating and fishing on the Caloosahatchee.

Right: **The Harold P. Curtis Honey Company is housed in the most colorful building in LaBelle. A mural stretches the length of the building and depicts Harold as a boy harvesting honey in the 1940s. Inside, customers can shop for a variety of honey products produced by the family.**

Below: **A colorful roadside produce stand near Alva. South Florida's warm sunny winter months are perfect for growing fresh vegetables.**

In the early 1900s, the river was spectacularly beautiful. Its slow, clear waters, alive with fish and manatees, flowed lazily below a canopy of mature oaks, pines, and palms that were home to a metropolis of egrets, herons, roseate spoonbills, and other wetland birds. In the 1930s, the river was "improved" by the Army Corps of Engineers, who straightened more than thirty of its oxbow curves.

Today, the environmental damage this caused is recognized, and an effort is underway to restore some of these curves and return the river to a more natural state. Nevertheless, the river today is lovely and filled with wildlife. The dark waters flow lazily between green banks, with homes and estates dotting the shoreline. The river is part of the cross-Florida Okeechobee Waterway, and a constant parade of pleasure boats of all sizes and shapes travel its length.

Heading east on Highway 78, the road traces the river, here and there offering tantalizing views of the waterway. A good place to enjoy some of the river's wild beauty is at Caloosahatchee River Regional Park, which offers miles of hiking and biking trails and plenty of places to sit and watch the lazy river roll by. About eight miles past the town of Alva, watch for a turn on Fort Denaud Bridge Road. The small bridge that crosses the river here is called a swing bridge because it is built to pivot on its center to allow boat traffic through. This is a very old design and there are only two of these bridges remaining in operation in Florida. This bridge was installed in 1963 when the channel here was widened, but the iron span itself is much older, dating to the 1920s when it spanned the intra-coastal waterway near Pompano Beach. If you have time, park at the bridge-tender's building, where you can sit and watch the fascinating operation of this bridge as boat traffic passes through. First the tender walks to the center of the bridge to start and engage the motors that swing the bridge open, then he remains (stranded on the bridge in midstream) until the traffic has passed and he shifts the gears to close the bridge.

The gracious little town of LaBelle was created by Captain Francis Asbury Hendry, known to all as "Berry," who set aside acreage in his cattle empire to plat the town and offered lots free to anyone who would build a house. Hendry named the town after his two daughters, Laura Jane and Carrie Belle. In his final years, he built a fine cracker-style house near the river that still stands today, and, while not open for tours, can be seen by driving to the sandy, shady end of Fraser Avenue.

The Caloosahachee River is part of a waterway that gives boaters a straight route across Florida, from the Atlantic Ocean to the Gulf of Mexico. The small marina in LaBelle offers free overnight dockage to weary mariners making the journey.

These days, downtown LaBelle is an up-and-coming destination for day-trippers from Fort Myers. They come to stroll the small downtown, shop for antiques, grab a hot cup of joe at Bridge Street Coffee and Tea, or have lunch at Forrey Grill or Two Peas. Easily the most colorful building in town is the Harold P. Curtis Honey Company, which features a stunning full-wall mural depicting Harold and his brother Elliot harvesting honey as boys. Inside, Harold's daughter Renee Curtis Pratt sells several types of natural raw honey, including Orange Blossom, Palmetto, Sea Grape, Mangrove, and Wildflower—all of which come from the Curtis's hives. Renee also offers tours when she has time, and if she is out running errands, the store is left open and customers serve themselves and pay on the honor system.

Curtis's honey store stands at one end of the town's high drawbridge crossing the river. A two-block stroll leads to the riverside Barron Park, which is a good place to sit and watch the river go by. Early in the century, sternwheelers and steamboats plied the navigable waters of the river, bringing travelers of all types to LaBelle. Henry Ford was one of these visitors, but his interest in the town was more than casual. During World War I, a shortage of rubber for tires had threatened the military effort and made the use of cars on the home front difficult.

Determined that America should have its own home-grown rubber supply, Ford, Edison, and their friend, tire magnate Harvey Firestone, had formed a company to develop alternate sources of rubber. Edison started by focusing on distilling rubber from common plants such as Giant Goldenrod at his estate in Fort Myers. When Ford acquired an eight-thousand-acre estate near LaBelle, he began to develop the property into a traditional rubber plantation. While the effort never became commercially viable, it made LaBelle and the surrounding area another favorite destination for "the famous friends." And it's not hard to see why.

Today, you can easily find a place to sit along a tranquil stretch of this beautiful river and enjoy the sounds of nature. And it doesn't take much imagination to picture the days when great oaks spread across the river, steamboats chugged along its slowly winding curves, and somewhere nearby the famous friends picnicked and planned the future of American industry.

---

## 9

# JUPITER ISLAND JAUNT

## JUPITER INLET LIGHTHOUSE TO STUART

*Begin at the Jupiter Inlet Lighthouse and Museum near the intersection of US Highway 1 and Florida State Route 811/A1A, just south of Beach Road in Jupiter. Head east on Beach Road (State Route A1A), which turns to the north up Jupiter Island to Blowing Rocks Preserve. Continue north to SE Bridge Road (County Road 708), and turn west (left) onto the mainland and then north (right) on SE Dixie Highway toward Port Salerno.*

*Turn east (right) on SE Salerno Road and turn left at the end of the road along the waterfront to the Fish House Art Center. Return to SE Dixie Highway and continue north into Stuart*

The elegant Jupiter Inlet Lighthouse rises 105 feet above the sport-fishing bustle of the harbor below. A great way to enjoy the lighthouse is to arrive near sunrise, park by the lighthouse, walk across the US Highway 1 bridge over the inlet, and head left into a small marina. There, a bench near the end of the marina gas dock is the perfect place to sit and watch the sun rise, illuminating the lighthouse as the inlet becomes busy with fishing boats heading out to hunt for the blue marlin and sailfish for which this coast is legendary.

This was a very different coast back in the 1850s when the lighthouse was being built. The nearest settlement was Titusville, almost one hundred miles away, and the heavy bricks for the lighthouse had to be laboriously offloaded

The graceful Jupiter Inlet Lighthouse overlooks one of the most beautiful small harbors on Florida's Atlantic coast. The lighthouse has been in operation since 1860.

from boats and dragged across sand and wetlands to reach the construction site. The laborers suffered disease and Indian attacks, but in 1860 the lighthouse was lit and its powerful beacon began warning ships away from the dangerous shoals offshore. If you want to visit the lighthouse and its accompanying museum, they open at 10:00 a.m. (closed Mondays in winter) and offer tours throughout the day.

A few miles up island, you will find Blowing Rocks Preserve. Owned by the Nature Conservancy, this seventy-three-acre site protects a long stretch of unblemished beach that is a favorite with nesting turtles. The beach is also unique for its long rock shelf that creates a rocks-and-surf landscape more reminiscent of Maine than Florida. The rock shelf is actually limestone formed from prehistoric shells. The constant pounding of waves has worn the rock into craggy shapes, and in places the surf sometimes explodes through holes, hence the park's name. Lena Kassak, who volunteered at the park for thirteen years before becoming a full-time employee, noted that "The

rock shelf is so pockmarked that sometimes the newly hatched baby turtles get stuck in the depressions, so we have turtle patrols that go along the shore and help them into the water."

The preserve's visitor's center on the bay side of the road is full of interesting displays on the ecology of the beach and the Indian River. From Blowing Rocks to the end of the island, the narrow road winds through some of the highest-priced real estate in North America. This was confirmed in 2006, when legendary golfer Tiger Woods paid $38 million for a ten-acre estate on the island, then turned around and bought the 1.7-acre neighboring parcel for $6.5 million. Roaming along the narrow State Route A1A is a trip through mile after mile of lush, tropical landscaping festooned with bougainvillea, hibiscus, jasmine, and exotic palms, offering frequent glimpses of water on both sides.

Surprisingly, many of the houses, when they can be seen at all, are small and ever-so-tasteful. The road turns and

This beautiful alley of banyan trees shades the access road onto northern Jupiter Island.

exits the island through a spectacular green alley of gigantic trees that form a dense canopy over the road. But if you are in the mood for another, longer beach walk, continue along North Beach Road to the entrance of Hobe Sound National Wildlife Refuge. The refuge's three miles of beach link with four more miles that are part of the St. Lucie Inlet Preserve State Park, offering one of the longest unbroken stretches of pristine Atlantic beach to be found in southern Florida.

When you've washed the sand off your feet and gotten back into your shoes, head to the mainland and turn north to Port Salerno. At the end of Port Salerno Road stands the Fish House Art Center, a charming facility that houses the studios of working artists, including ceramic tile, sculpture, glass, fiber, and several fine art painters.

The center is the brainchild of physician and sailor John Hennessee and artist Beverly Ervin. Artists are invited to share these dreamlike studio spaces based on the quality of their work. Also here is the Art Gumbo Gallery that shows the work of many top area artists, as well as a gourmet coffee shop that offers a great place to relax, sip quality java, and enjoy the view of the boat-filled harbor.

More galleries await in Stuart, whose delightfully restored historic downtown is full of inviting restaurants and shops. Walk around the town and admire the colorful murals, sparkling fountains, and street-side art. This is a great place to find lunch or dinner. Afterward, buy an ice cream cone and walk down Flagler Avenue to visit the old Stuart Feed Supply Store, which has been lovingly restored and houses the Stuart Heritage Museum. After exploring the museum's unique collection of memorabilia, you can step into the waterfront park beside the museum, pick a

Above: **A brown pelican relaxes on a pier piling overlooking Jupiter Inlet.**

Opposite: **Blowing Rocks Reserve features a wave-sculpted limestone shore, one of the few rocky coastlines in the state.**

bench, and spend some time imagining what this coast might have looked like in 1900, when the shore was lined with fishing boats and pineapple farmers could be heard haggling with the merchants of Flagler Avenue.

# PART II

# CENTRAL FLORIDA

Opened in 1947, the mermaid shows at Weeki Wachee are still one of Florida's most popular attractions.

Locals like to say that central Florida offers some of the state's best features, including fabulous beaches on two coasts, warm tropical winter weather, and rolling green landscapes in the heartland. And pastoral it is, particularly around Reedy Lake, Lake Wales, and the rest of the chain of sparkling blue lakes that lie nestled among hills where the soil is perfect for growing oranges.

In springtime, the hills are blanketed with orchards that burst forth with citrus blossoms, perfuming the air with a heady fragrance. In winter, a drive along country roads here can lead through mile after mile of deep green orchards laden with sweet oranges. Walt Disney spotted the beauty of this land when he bought twenty-seven thousand acres outside the then-tiny town of Orlando for his new Disney World in the 1960s. Today, the Orlando area is one of the fastest-growing regions in the state. However, you can still find plenty of inviting backroads that lead to small, charming towns and out-of-the-way attractions here. Outside Lake Wales, the romantically lovely Art Deco Bok Tower, surrounded by picturesque gardens, rises two hundred feet above the highest point of land for miles around. Off-the-beaten-path towns such as Micanopy and Mount Dora have elegantly restored historic districts brimming with antique shops, boutiques, and restaurants. Along the east coast, the stunning beaches at Canaveral National Seashore are perfect places to walk for miles along the sandy shore, wade in the surf, commune with salt marsh wildlife, and perhaps get a chance to see the smoke-and-thunder spectacle of a space launch. Farther south, timeless barrier strands like Orchid and Hutchinson's islands are home to protected beaches where sea turtles come ashore in droves to lay eggs and where silver coins from centuries-old Spanish shipwrecks still occasionally wash ashore after a storm.

The spirit of the Old West lives on along Florida State Route 64, which follows the nineteenth-century route that Florida cowboys, known as "crackers," took as they led their steers to market. And north of Tampa, the cave-riddled bedrock of limestone that stretches for miles is home to some of the world's largest, purest, and most beautiful freshwater springs. At Homosassa, you can stand in a room below water level and watch through a window as wild manatees, once thought to be the mermaids of legend, feed and lazily cavort in the warm, clear water. At Weeki Wachee Springs, mermaids of the human variety still perform the daily underwater ballet that has captivated audiences for forty years and has made the springs synonymous with the fanciful roadside attractions that once were found along backroads from one end of Florida to the other.

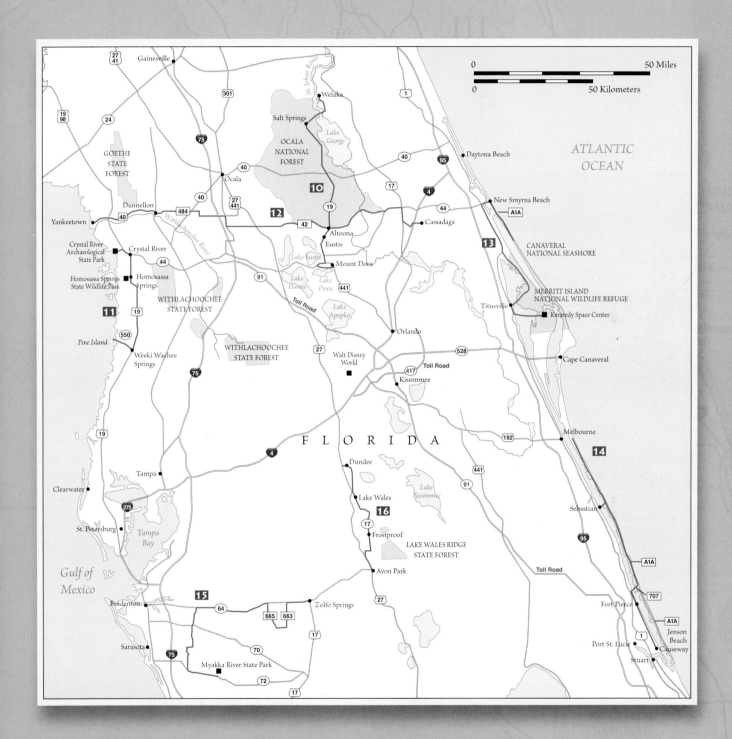

# 10

# SALT SPRINGS and STEAM TRAINS

## MOUNT DORA TO WELAKA

*Starting in downtown Mount Dora, follow Old US Highway 441/County Road 500A north and west along the north shore of Lake Dora. Turn left onto Lakeshore Drive/County Road 452, and continue along the north side of Lake Dora. In Tavares, County Road 452 turns north (right) and becomes North St. Clair Abrams Avenue. Turn northeast (right) onto East Burleigh Boulevard and continue to the intersection with Lake Eustis Drive and turn left. The road is still County Road 452 and becomes Lakeshore Drive as it heads north along the shores of Lake Eustis. Follow the road into Eustis and turn north (left) onto State Route 19. Drive north into Ocala National Forest. Turn east (right) on County Road 445 and drive for about five miles to Alexander Springs. Return to Route 19 and continue north to Salt Springs.*

*Just north of Salt Springs, turn east (right) on Cemetery Road (gravel) and follow the signs to the Fort Gates Ferry. Take the car ferry across the river, and follow the main streets through tiny Fruitland to County Road 309 and head north (left) into Welaka.*

Mount Dora's vintage train takes visitors on a scenic journey along the shores of Lake Dora. Both the city and lake were named for a hardy pioneer woman who provided meals for surveyors working in the area in the 1840s.

If there was an award for most charming country town in Florida, Mount Dora might win it. Located on a ridge above Lake Dora, the town and its blue waters were named for Dora Anne Drowdy, a hardy pioneer woman who homesteaded here in the mid-1800s. As the story goes, she provided lodging, home-cooked meals, and hospitality to a group of surveyors working in the area in 1847. They were so thankful that they named the lake in her honor. The town developed later, and the lovely location among the rolling hills and lakes made it a magnet for northerners who came to escape the cold and enjoy hunting and fishing in the region. At some point, "Mount" became part of the town's name to acknowledge its whopping altitude of 184 feet above sea level. The town also was part of the Chautauqua circuit, receiving a regular roster of top speakers and entertainers, which increased its status.

Today, Mount Dora continues to attract visitors with a maze of charming shops and restaurants downtown. Built in 1883, the elegant Lakeside Inn still serves guests iced tea or frosty lemonade on the shady porch where rocking chairs offer a genteel respite. Among the famous guests have been Thomas Edison and President Calvin Coolidge. A short stroll leads to the town's restored Victorian-era train station. A train still runs from here, taking visitors on a short but scenic three-and-a-half-mile jaunt around the lake. Normally, the train is pulled by a small diesel engine, but from time to time the train operator borrows a period steam engine, which makes the trip even more authentic.

Left: **Mount Dora offers an abundance of interesting shops and restaurants.**
Right: **Roadside citrus stands like this one can still be found throughout southern and central Florida.**

Several boat tours also operate from the waterfront. One of the most popular tours leads from Mount Dora to neighboring Tavares along the short but hauntingly beautiful Dora Canal. This canal was never logged and is lined with a captivating watery forest of towering cypress trees, giving the landscape a primeval feel.

From Mount Dora, this route follows the pretty shores of Lake Dora and Lake Eustis, offering a chance to explore the less commercial but interesting towns of Tavares and Eustis, which, along with Mount Dora, call themselves the "Golden Triangle" of Florida's lake region.

In Eustis, you'll connect with Florida State Route 19 and head north into Ocala National Forest. A prime place for bird watching and hiking, this is also a favorite destination for swimmers who come during hot Florida summers to cool off in one of the many crystalline blue springs. The springs remain at a constant 72° to 74°F. Due to their popularity, many of Florida's springs have been surrounded with concrete walkways, but one that has largely escaped that fate is Alexander Springs. Aside from a campground at one end, this spring looks much like it must have a thousand years ago. The vibrant blue pool is bordered with tropical foliage and filled with fish, making it a favorite with snorkelers. The spring also marks the beginning of a popular seven-mile-long paddling route.

Farther north, Salt Springs was named for its salt content, which apparently is acquired as the water bubbles up through a layer of salt deposits left by an ancient sea. More developed than Alexander Springs, it is nonetheless pretty and a popular place for picnics, snorkeling, and family gatherings.

Just north of the little town of Salt Springs, you'll head right on the unpaved Cemetery Road, which leads through a maze of well-graded backcountry dirt roads to the tiny and wonderfully idiosyncratic Fort Gates Ferry. The ferry has a long and fascinating history. It began service in 1847 to transport soldiers to and from Fort Gates, which stood on the bank of the river during the Seminole Wars. Today, drivers arriving on the west bank pull up on the dock and turn on their headlights to signal that they want to cross. Powered by a tiny tugboat that was built from a 1918 sharpie sailboat, the barge-style ferry holds exactly two cars on the journey across the St. Johns River. The ferry ride lasts about ten minutes, costs ten dollars, and provides a scenic and historic experience as well as a practical one, cutting about fifty miles off the paved route north to cross the St. Johns River by bridge. On the far side of the river lies the quiet little hamlet of Welaka and the Welaka National Fish Hatchery and Aquarium. This small building contains rows of aquariums displaying many of Florida's

Above: The tiny Fort Gates Ferry takes two cars at a time across the St. Johns River. It has been in operation since 1847.

Left: Small wetlands like this cypress swamp near Mount Dora are an important part of Florida's unique ecosystem.

favorite sport fish, from largemouth bass and gar to the uniquely Southern pan fish known as stumpknockers. Signage provides information on each fish and the efforts of the hatchery to raise them. Of course after visiting, you may feel compelled to spend some time on the black-water banks of the St. Johns River with a fishing pole, some bait, a stocked cooler, and a comfortable chair.

# 11

# MANATEES and MERMAIDS

## CRYSTAL RIVER ARCHAEOLOGICAL STATE PARK TO PINE ISLAND

*Beginning at Crystal River Archaeological State Park, turn east (right) on State Park Street as you leave the park. Then turn south (right) on US Highway 19 and drive through Homosassa Springs to the entrance of Homosassa Springs Wildlife State Park on the right. After visiting the park, continue south on US Highway 19 to just past the intersection of State Route 50 and turn right into Weeki Wachee Springs. Return north on US Highway 19, and almost immediately turn west (left) on County Road 550/Cortez Boulevard to the intersection with Pine Island Drive. There, turn north (right) on Pine Island Drive and follow it as it heads west into Pine Island.*

Even on busy days, Crystal River Archaeological State Park is a place of serenity. Here, paths lead below moss-draped oaks to the river where two mounds rise forty-five feet into the air. A staircase leads to the top of one of the mounds, where the view up and down the river is impressive. These high mounds are testament to the long-vanished civilization of the Calusa Indians and are some of the best-preserved shell mounds in the state. These mounds were built from uncountable quantities of oyster shells and other refuse cast off over hundreds, even thousands, of years. The Calusa chiefs built their dwellings and important temples on the summits of these mounds, which were the only safe ground above hurricane flood levels.

Set atop limestone bedrock riddled with water-filled caverns, this part of west central Florida is home to some of the world's most impressive and purest freshwater springs. Homosassa Springs is one of the largest of these, producing millions of gallons of clear pure water hourly at a consistent 72°F. For West Indian manatees who cannot survive below 68°F, this is warm compared to the ocean's chilly wintertime temperatures, making this one of their preferred winter resorts.

The manatees arrive like clockwork each winter, as do the tourists who come to see them. Some manatees are here for extended stays because they have been specifically brought here for rehabilitation after being injured in the wild. A net across the mouth of the springs keeps these sea cows in the park and separate from the sizable population of wild manatees that winter in the river just outside.

The key attraction at Homosassa Springs is the underwater observatory, where you can watch the resident manatees slowly swimming in the deepest part of the springs.

A kayaker paddles the iridescent blue pools of Homosassa Springs.

Thousands of fish are here, too, including mullet, snook, and the occasional gar. From the walkways around the spring you can sometimes see manatees sleeping in the shallows and watch as they lift their heads every five minutes or so to take a breath, apparently without waking up. Be sure to see one

Above: Visitors aboard a tour boat at Homosassa Springs get a glimpse into the wild, natural paradise of a first-magnitude spring. Herons, egrets, manatees, and a host of other birds and wildlife are all drawn to this remarkable ecosystem.

Left: In winter, manatees gather in the warm waters of many of Florida's crystalline springs. This manatee is enjoying watching the tourists at Homosassa Springs.

of the feeding demonstrations. The manatees, knowing they are going to be fed goodies like carrots and sweet potatoes, will gather by the bleachers along the bank about thirty minutes before show time. The volunteers who feed them are a font of knowledge about these animals, making this an informative and delightful show.

Just outside the park, tour operators bring groups of swimmers to snorkel with the wild manatees in the river. Nearby, volunteers in kayaks make sure that swimmers only reach out to touch these gentle creatures with one hand and only after the animal has approached them.

Manatees were once thought to be the mermaids of ancient sailors' legends, but as an old joke goes, if that's the case, these sailors had probably been at sea a very long time. Those sailors would have probably preferred the "mermaids" found at Weeki Wachee Springs, twenty miles south of Homosassa. Weeki Wachee, where daily mermaid shows are held, is synonymous with the roadside

## A TREASURE OF OLD FLORIDA

In 1946, a former Navy frogman named Newton Perry had a wild idea for a business. What if pretty girls used air hoses instead of scuba tanks to breath underwater while doing ballet-like aquatic routines? Would tourists pay to see something like that? With little more than an idea, he scouted around for a site, settling on Weeki Wachee Springs for his enterprise. His first job was to clean out the spring and remove the wrecked cars and junk that filled it. He then built an eighteen-seat theater below water level where visitors could look through a window directly into the sparkling clear waters of the spring and watch the mermaids cavort.

Then, as now, the mermaids were mostly local girls who were trained to swim underwater, breathe through air hoses, and perform such unique underwater tasks as eating bananas and drinking soda. In addition to the mermaid show, Weeki Wachee featured a river cruise, orchid gardens, and a beach created from river sand.

The mermaid show at Weeki Wachi Springs

In the early days, attendance was low, but as word got out visitors began arriving in droves. In 1959, the park was purchased by ABC, and the subsequent publicity (along with the addition of professional-level staging, props, and choreography) turned Weeki Wachee Springs into Florida's top tourist attraction. ABC expanded the theater to five hundred seats and presented eight shows a day. Celebrities like Elvis Presley came to see the show, and the glamour of being a mermaid drew applicants from around the world.

While mermaids often traveled extensively as ambassadors for the park and for Florida, the work of being a mermaid was extremely demanding and sometimes dangerous. Even today there is a strong sisterhood among mermaids, past and present. The saying is "Once a mermaid, always a mermaid."

Sadly, competition from Disney World, which opened in 1971, impacted Weeki Wachee Springs. Attendance dropped and revenues suffered. More recently, an argument with the powerful Florida Water Management District over the manmade beach threatened to close the facility, raising cries of despair from people of all ages across the country who consider the Weeki Wachee mermaid show an indispensable part of Florida history.

Fortunately, another powerful entity, the Florida State Parks, stepped in and took over the park in 2008. With plans for improving the park and promises that the mermaid show will continue, the future looks bright for young girls everywhere who dream of being a real Weeki Wachee mermaid.

**Sunset illuminates the harbor at Crystal River.**

attractions that were part of every Florida vacation in the years before Disney World opened in 1971. Of course, these mermaids are beautiful young women who perform under water thanks to an air tube system created by ex-navy frogman Newton Perry, who developed the attraction in 1946. During the attraction's heyday in the 1950s, a dozen or more mermaids would sit along a wall that separated the springs from the then-sleepy US Highway 19 and flip their tails to entice visitors into the park. The park's fortunes have ebbed and flowed in the ensuing years, but Weeki Wachee Springs was added to Florida's state park system in 2008, ensuring that this historic bit of Old Florida will continue for years to come.

Near Weeki Wachee, a small side road leads through coastal marshes to Pine Island. This tiny settlement is home to a handful of vacation cottages and the finest public beach in the area. Naturalists will like this area for the network of dike roads that lead through the wetlands between Pine Island and Bayport to the south. Find a place to park and you can walk or bike for miles along these roads lined on both side with salt ponds, home to a number of birds, including herons, wood storks, and egrets.

# 12

# PSYCHICS, SALT MARSHES,
# and FLORIDA'S UNKNOWN HIGHWAY

### CASSADAGA TO YANKEETOWN

*Start in Cassadaga and head west on Cassadaga Road to Dr. Martin L. King Jr. Boulevard/County Road 4101, and turn south (left). At the junction with State Route 472, turn left again and follow Route 472 to the junction of US Highway 17, where you'll head north (right) on Highway 17/92 into downtown DeLand. When leaving DeLand, turn west (left) onto State Route 44. At the intersection with State Route 42, turn west (right), and then turn north (right) at the intersection with County Road 475 to County Road 484/SE 132nd Street. When you reach County Road 484, turn west (left). Just before Interstate 75, at SW 16th Avenue, turn south (left) to Don Garlits Museum. Return to County Road 484 and turn west (left). In Dunnellon, turn north (right) on US Highway 41, and watch for Rainbow Springs State Park on the right. After visiting it, return to Dunnellon and turn west (right) on Pennsylvania Avenue for a short distance. Then turn north (right) on Cedar Street, which becomes County Road 40 as it curves and heads to Yankeetown.*

If you would like to know how this trip is going to turn out before you take it, the best place to start is in the little town of Cassadaga—the self-proclaimed world capital of psychics. Cassadaga has been a mystical town since 1875, when New Yorker George Colby, following three "spirit guides," arrived to found the Cassadaga Spiritualist Camp. Today, the fifty-five-acre encampment is the hub of a small town that has grown up around it.

Within the encampment, tidy frame houses stand on quiet streets, many sporting small, tasteful signs advertising spiritual readings and healing. There are plenty to choose from, as the camp's official roster lists about fifty psychics. Newcomers are welcome, and the camp maintains an active schedule of church services and activities, from spiritual healings and classes to bingo. On Thursdays, Fridays, and Saturdays, visitors can take a guided tour of this historic spiritual community at 2:00 p.m.

The next stop on this route is DeLand, originally named Persimmon Hollow. In the mid-1800s, New Yorker Henry DeLand visited here and fell so in love with the warm pastoral beauty of the place that he rushed home, closed out his affairs, and returned to buy a large tract of land. One of his first undertakings was the creation of DeLand Academy, which is now Stetson University, the oldest continually operating university in Florida.

Anchored by its stunning copper-domed county courthouse, DeLand's downtown is charming. Its streets are

A street sign reflects Cassadaga's roots as a spiritualist community. Founded in 1895, the village is still home to many practicing spiritualists and mediums.

Top: A scenic country road winds through the lush farmland of central Florida.

Below left: In early spring, orange trees hang heavy with fruit, while the blossoms that promise next year's harvest perfume the air with their heady scent. This tree is in an orchard near the tiny town of Altoona.

Below right: A statue of an angel watches over the yard of a Cassadaga resident. A nearby sign advertises spiritual readings.

Spring wildflowers decorate a rolling farm field north of Orlando.

lined with turn-of the-century buildings chock full of restaurants and boutiques, as well as antique and gift shops.

From DeLand, State Route 42 wanders for a delightful fifty-four miles through the scenic heartland of central Florida. Cattle-ranching is the third-largest agricultural industry in Florida, after citrus and sugar, and it shows here. Well-tended ranches spread across the gently rolling landscape. In between the beef ranches are even more prosperous-looking horse farms with immaculate barns, stables, and postcard-perfect green paddocks surrounded by miles of white fences. Horses are serious business in these parts. Just east of the rush of Interstate 75 stands the Don Garlits Museum, which pays tribute to the king of drag racing in the 1950s, 1960s, and 1970s. This museum is actually two: one tells the story of the development of drag racing from its earliest days and the other showcases Garlits's own spectacular collection of antique and classic automobiles. These range from a mostly wood 1904 Orient Buckboard to superbly restored muscle cars of the 1960s and 1970s.

If you are looking for a place to spend a few pleasant hours in nature, the crystalline waters of Rainbow Springs lie just north of County Road 484 on US Highway 41. This stunning aqua-blue spring is part of the Rainbow Springs State Park. Here, in a pastoral setting that is hugely popular with local families, you can cook up a meal at a barbecue pit, put on your bathing suit and swim in the clear, green waters, or rent a kayak to explore this gorgeous environment at your leisure.

The waters of the Rainbow River flow south from here to join the black-water Withlacoochee River at Dunnellon. One of the first things you notice about Dunnellon is that the shady streets are lined with many fine Victorian and early twentieth-century homes. The wealth that created these homes and some of the elegant buildings downtown came from the town's long and sometimes dark history as the nation's premier mining source of phosphates. In the early days of the mine, the mine owners grew rich while the largely black miners worked long hours for a pittance. The miners would come into the bars and bawdy houses of

Dunnellon on payday to blow off steam, and things often got wild. The shooting of two white merchants by two black miners in 1895 led to an unprecedented string of shootings and lynchings.

Today none of Dunnellon's rough past is evident, and although it is not touristy, the downtown is home to restaurants and gift shops that invite visitors to stop and explore.

Along the two-hundred-mile curve of the Gulf Coast between Tarpon Springs and Apalachicola, there are few beaches. Instead, thousands of square miles of land seem to merge with the sea in vast salt marshes that are nurseries and incubators for a dazzling array of birds, fish, and wildlife. It is not for nothing that the local tourism folks have dubbed this the Nature Coast.

The transition from farmland to salt marsh starts at Yankeetown. Yankeetown is the kind of salty, unrepentant fishing town with a rough-hewn charm that attracts characters and those who wish to live away from the madding crowd. Along the sandy roads here, old cedar cottages all seem to sport a shallow-draft fishing boat in the yard. Local anglers frequent the vast coastal scrub and wetlands of Waccasassa Bay State Preserve, encompassing almost twenty miles of coastline accessible only by boat. In fact, it often seems that every other person you run into here is a fishing guide or runs tours into the endless realm of shallow wetlands where time is set by the ebb and flow of the tides.

## 13

# The WILD CANAVERAL COAST

KENNEDY SPACE CENTER VISITOR COMPLEX TO CANAVERAL NATIONAL SEASHORE

*Begin at the Kennedy Space Center Visitor Complex, and drive west on Florida Highway 405/Nasa Parkway W across the causeway to US Highway 1/Florida A1A/Washington Avenue, and turn north (right). Continue into historic downtown Titusville, and then drive north along US Highway 1 to the intersection with Max Brewer Memorial Parkway (also Titusville Road and State Route 406). Turn east (right) to cross the causeway into Merritt Island National Wildlife Refuge. At the Y intersection, bear left on State Route 406 to the one-way Black Point Wildlife Drive and turn left. Follow the road until it returns to State Route 406, where you'll turn left. At the intersection with Kennedy Parkway/State Route 3, turn north (left) and continue north when the road becomes US Highway 1. Turn east (right) onto County Road A1A in New Smyrna Beach, and continue east across the causeway and then south (right) along the coast into Canaveral National Seashore.*

If you were an astronaut and could gaze northward through the window of your space shuttle standing high above its launch pad at Kennedy Space Center, you would have a superb view of one of the most pristine stretches of coastline in Florida. That such a bastion of technology exists at the wild edge of Canaveral National Seashore and Merritt Island National Wildlife Refuge is just one of the many interesting contrasts for which Florida is famous.

Fortunately, you don't have to be an astronaut to explore the world of NASA and space travel. The Kennedy Space Center Visitor Complex is a scientific, theme-park-style experience that leads visitors through the history of space exploration, from the earliest days of unmanned satellites,

to the Apollo and Space Shuttle programs, and into the future—with a look at upcoming manned Mars expeditions. This is a wonderful place for children and adults alike to be inspired by seemingly limitless possibilities of science and technology. It is also a huge facility, and you can easily spend an entire day exploring it. Among the don't-miss attractions are the *Atlantis* Space Shuttle (veteran of thirty-three space missions) and the guided bus tour of the Space Center. The tour takes you to view the launch facilities and the huge Apollo/Saturn V exhibit building which contains a 363-foot-long Saturn V rocket, as well as a moon rock you can touch and numerous exhibits on the Apollo-era missions.

Above: **A narrow road traces a tantalizing line along the shifting sands of Canaveral National Seashore.**

Right: **An antique gas pump stands outside a service station near Titusville.**

The nearby town of Titusville is another surprise, albeit a quieter one. The two-block downtown features charming rows of early twentieth-century commercial buildings that house an eclectic collection of galleries, restaurants, and shops. A sure bet here is the Café Chocolat, a decadently inviting chocolateria. Next door is a neighborhood favorite—Pistilli's Pizza and Bistro—and across the street Playalinda Brewery serves up chilly craft beers with names like "Go Big" and "Rocket Man Red."

Turning right just north of downtown Titusville, you quickly leave civilization behind as you enter Merritt Island National Wildlife Refuge. The combination of salt and freshwater marshes found along this protected spit of land are home to over five hundred species of birds and animals, including snowy egrets, bald eagles, wood storks, and the brilliantly hued roseate spoonbills. The refuge is also home to the largest wintertime population of West Indian manatees on Florida's eastern seaboard. These lumbering and gentle animals, also known as sea cows, swim and raise their young in the warm, shallow waters of the lagoon.

Left: **The Rocket Garden at the Kennedy Space Center Visitor Complex displays many of the most important launch vehicles of the American space program, including Mercury-Redstone, Titan II, Atlas-Agena, and Saturn 1B rockets.**

Right: **Space Shuttle *Atlantis* is the veteran of thirty-three space missions and has flown more than 126 million miles.**

The most popular way to enjoy the refuge is to drive or bicycle along the seven-mile, one-way Black Point Wildlife Drive, which meanders through a labyrinth of salt and freshwater marshes, offering numerous places to pull over and view the birds that congregate here. There are also several hiking trails that wind through the refuge and are particularly popular in fall, winter, and early spring, when the mosquitoes are less active.

Heading north, if there is one thing New Smyrna Beach is not, it is new. The Timucuan Indians lived here for thousands of years. In the 1600s, Spanish friars did missionary work all along this coast, and in 1632 the Spanish cleared the Kings Road between New Smyrna and St. Augustine, creating one of the earliest roads in the New World.

After the Spanish ceded Florida to the British, Scottish Lord Turnbull established a colony of 1,200 Greeks and Turks in New Smyrna that lasted for ten years before disease, Indian attacks, and harsh treatment by Turnbull's agents forced the survivors to retreat to St. Augustine. Today, New Smyrna Beach is a charming and somewhat undiscovered waterfront community with a sense of timelessness that makes it a fine place to park yourself for a day, a week, or a year.

Crossing over from the mainland to the beach and heading south, the beach town fracas will vanish as you enter the sandy realm of Canaveral National Seashore. This amazingly unspoiled twenty-three miles of beach is a secret national treasure. Even on hot summer days, there are rarely more than a handful of beachgoers present, making it easy to find a stretch of sand you can call your own.

Cape Canaveral is one of the oldest geographic names in North America. It was first used in 1513, when explorer Ponce de Leon claimed this land for Spain. As the Indian River citrus industry exploded in the late 1800s, small towns emerged along the waterway. One of these towns was Eldora, which flourished for a while as a fruit-shipping and trade center and then faded away. Today, all that remains of Eldora is the Eldora State House, a well-preserved frame building that presides over the historic town site near the north end of Canaveral National Seashore. Also nearby is Turtle Mound, the remains of a shell mound that was probably created by the Timucuan people thousands of years ago. Aside from these small mementos of past civilizations, the park is best appreciated for its natural beauty. And appreciate it you will, especially if you take a walk along the beach—past the cadre of surf fishermen into the realm of sand and surf, where shorebirds scamper along the ever-shifting sands and pelicans glide above the curling waves.

Top: A surf fisher tries her luck in the early morning light at Canaveral National Seashore.

Below left: A great blue heron hunts patiently in the quiet waters of Merritt Island Wildlife Refuge.

Below right: A colorful display outside an antique shop in Titusville.

# 14

# The TREASURE COAST

## MELBOURNE BEACH TO JENSEN BEACH CAUSEWAY

*From Melbourne Beach, head south on County Road A1A to Sebastian Inlet State Recreation Area. About three miles past the Sebastian Inlet State Park Bridge, turn right onto the Historic Jungle Trail to reach the Pelican Island National Wildlife Refuge. Then continue to Wabasso Road/County Road 510 and turn west (right) to cross the Indian River Lagoon. Turn north (right) on US Highway 1 into Sebastian and watch for Indian River Drive on the right.*

*Follow it to Mel Fisher's Treasure Museum (on the right). Return across the Wabasso Causeway on Wabasso Road and turn south (right) on County Road A1A. Near Fort Pierce, County A1A turns and crosses the Indian River Lagoon to the mainland connecting with US Highway 1 in Fort Pierce.*

*Turn south (left) on US Highway 1 to Orange Avenue/State Route 68, and go a short distance east (left) and turn south (right) on Indian River Drive. Follow Indian River Drive to Jensen Beach Causeway just north of Stuart. Turn east (left) and cross the causeway, turning south (right) on County Road A1A to continue south to MacArthur Boulevard. From there, turn east (left) and when the road runs close to the beach, watch on the left for Gilbert's Bar House of Refuge.*

For two rare species of sea turtles, the unbroken ribbon of beach that lies between Melbourne and Wabasso is the most important stretch of coastline in the Western Hemisphere. About 30 percent of all loggerhead turtles and green sea turtles in the United States come ashore to nest along this twenty-mile stretch of sand. Back in the 1950s, Archie Carr, a Florida herpetologist and conservationist, was one of the first to recognize the plight of sea

Above: **A fisherman casts his net into the still waters of Indian River, near Sebastian Inlet State Park.**

Opposite: **This narrow lane that winds along the Indian River on Orchid Island is one of the last of the historic shell roads that were once common byways in coastal Florida.**

Above: Blue skies and clouds reflect in the mirror-like waters of the Pelican Island National Wildlife Refuge.

Right: This walkway at Pelican Island National Wildlife Refuge is inscribed with the names of every National Wildlife Refuge in the United States and the year it was created. Established in 1903, Pelican Island was the first National Wildlife Refuge in the system.

turtles, whose very existence was threatened by the coastal development that disrupted the beaches they needed for nesting. Carr pioneered methods of turtle conservation, and today the Archie Carr National Wildlife Reserve continues the work he started.

The reserve is not one piece of land but a patchwork of public beaches and individual lots purchased as they become available. Eventually, conservationists hope that more than nine miles of the busiest nesting area will be protected. Turtles and their well-being are a passion of islanders and visitors alike along this shore, and every year volunteers turn out by the score to participate in the turtle watches, assist nesting mother turtles, and, later in the year, help the hatchlings in their dash to the sea.

One of the best public beaches in the area for enjoying sun, surf, and sand is the Sebastian Inlet State Recreation Area, which straddles both sides of Sebastian Inlet. This park is particularly popular with saltwater anglers who fish from the park jetties and with bird-watchers who enjoy the multitude of wading and shore birds found both on the sandy beach and on the quiet lagoon side. Surfers also come to ride the beach's famous waves.

Once you cross the inlet bridge, you are on Orchid Island, whose romantic name comes from the wild orchids that hung in festoons from the trees in pioneer days. The island is special in many respects, not the least of which are the silver pieces of eight that occasionally wash up on the beach here. It was along this shore that the legendary Spanish Plate Fleet of 1715 sank in a hurricane. Two and a half centuries later, in the 1960s, treasure hunters Kip Wagner and Mel Fisher recovered thousands of coins here, as well as gold and silver bars, jewelry, and a wealth of artifacts.

Today, visitors can see some of that treasure at the McLarty Treasure Museum, located at the south end of Sebastian Inlet State Recreation Area. The museum features displays and artifacts that tell the story of the 1715 fleet and the treasure hunting that has taken place along this

## SPANISH PLATE FLEET OF 1715

In 1714, Spain's long war with England ended. For years, the Spanish king had not dared to allow his fleets to carry gold and silver from the New World for fear of being plundered. As hostilities ended, the gold-starved monarch sent a large fleet out to return with the huge stockpile of gold and silver that had been accumulating for years in Havana and South America. In July of 1715, a fleet of twelve ships set sail from Havana for Spain. On board was an unprecedented treasure of silver and gold bars, chests of coins, gems, and jewelry, as well as 2,500 men, women, and children who had waited years for safe passage to Spain.

*Urca de Lima* by William Trotter depicts one of the Spanish ships destroyed in a hurricane in 1715. *Courtesy of the artist*

Pressure to reach Europe quickly forced Captain-General Don Juan Esteban de Ubilla to order the fleet to sail during hurricane season. It was a decision he would soon regret. Just five days later, along the Florida coast, the fleet encountered a storm whose winds quickly grew to over one hundred miles per hour. One by one, the ships succumbed to the hurricane's fury and were dashed to pieces on the merciless shore.

The next day 1,500 bedraggled survivors gathered and took stock. They were on a hostile shore, far from any settlement. A group set out for Havana in a small open boat that was made serviceable to request rescue. Eventually, ships from Havana and later St. Augustine did arrive, and the women and children were evacuated.

However, the men remained under orders to salvage as much treasure as possible.

Because the ships had sunk in shallow water, a great deal of treasure was recovered. But news of the disaster had reached far and wide, and soon pirate Henry Jennings from nearby Jamaica, encouraged by the island's English governor, descended and raided the beach party, making off with a considerable amount of treasure. He was so pleased with his success that he returned months later and raided the camp again, making off with another fortune.

The Spanish remained for more than three years and eventually recovered about half the original treasure. The rest remained on the bottom of the sea until the 1960s, when a contractor named Kip Wagner began investigating legends of coins washing up on the beach, leading to one of the largest treasure hunts of all time.

The small McLarty Treasure Museum on Orchid Island tells the historic and archaeological story of the 1715 fleet and features numerous artifacts recovered from the ships, along with few pieces of the actual treasure. To see a much more dazzling portion of the treasure, you have to visit Mel Fisher's Treasure Museum across the Wabasso Causeway in Sebastian. Here, gold and silver coins and bars, as well as gold religious artifacts, jewelry, and other valuables, fill the display cases. While smaller than the Mel Fisher Maritime Museum in Key West, this collection still packs a punch, and many of the items on display are for sale. A superbly crafted diamond-encrusted filigree jewelry set can be had for a mere $800,000. Less expensive are handcrafted pendants and necklaces made from gold doubloons and silver coins recovered from shipwrecks.

shore for almost three hundred years. The museum itself is built on the site where the survivors of the 1715 disaster, along with reinforcements from St. Augustine, labored for months to recover as much of the treasure as possible. A short distance south of the McLarty, a small sand road leads to Pelican Island National Wildlife Refuge, which lies along the Indian River Lagoon. The lagoon stretches for more than one hundred miles along the Florida coast between the mainland and the barrier islands and is one of the most biologically diverse estuaries in the world.

Pelican Island is a small strip of land sitting just off Orchid Island in the lagoon. In the 1890s, this was the last Atlantic Florida nesting site of the brown pelican, and in 1903 President Theodore Roosevelt signed a law designating Pelican Island a federally protected bird sanctuary, the first of what would become the nation's network of national wildlife refuges.

Today, Pelican Island National Wildlife Refuge is a popular site with bird-watchers who come to see egrets, numerous herons, and other wading birds, as well as roseate spoonbills in summer. Visitors can travel hiking trails that lead around salt marsh impoundments and the Centennial Boardwalk, which leads to a viewing tower overlooking the nesting islands in the Indian River Lagoon. The boardwalk was added at the one hundredth anniversary of the national wildlife refuge system, and the name of each national wildlife refuge and the year it was added to the system is engraved on the floor planks. The very first plank, of course, is Pelican Island.

The road that leads into the refuge is one of Orchid Island's little-known treasures. Called the Jungle Trail, it was originally built around 1920, and islanders have fought fiercely to save it from development. The simple, sandy byway leads beyond the refuge for several miles through the island's dense native growth, skirting housing developments that at times loom close, and winding along the tranquil waters of Indian River Lagoon. Along the way, it passes a small-frame house set on a wide, well-tended lawn that probably looks much now as it did fifty years ago. This is Richard and Mary Jones's home. Richard's grandfather homesteaded on Orchid Island in 1891, and Richard was born here in 1919. Like his grandfather before him, Richard raised grapefruit on this sixteen-acre farm for years. Most of the fruit was sold directly to fine restaurants,

A colorful handmade sign marks the home of Dick and Mary Jones. Dick's grandfather was among the area's original homesteaders, moving to Orchid Island and establishing a citrus farm here in 1891.

This lovely waterfront park in Fort Pierce is the perfect place to spend a cool Florida morning.

shipped abroad, or sold from the family's fruit stand. Jones sold the property to the state in 2008, and the Jones Pier Conservation Area was established. The main pier and small dock have been restored, and plans are in place to restore the fruit stand as well. A small cottage on the property will become a visitor's center to display historical artifacts and information about the homestead, and later a walking trail will be constructed.

The route jogs onto the mainland and becomes down-right urban as it passes through Fort Pierce. However, the town's waterfront park is a delight, with sculptures, fountains, inviting benches, and swaying palm trees that frame splendid views of the bay's turquoise waters. It's also well worthwhile to visit the nearby Manatee Observation Center, as well as the museum dedicated to gifted local artist A. E. "Bean" Backus, who was Florida's first interna-tionally recognized landscape painter.

South of Fort Pierce, the narrow, two-lane Indian River Drive was originally part of the Dixie Highway. Built in the 1920s, this road follows the shores of the Indian River Lagoon. In recent years, development has been forbidden on the water side, so from Fort Pierce to Stuart this is one of the most pleasantly scenic roads in the state. Drive slowly and enjoy the views.

Just north of Stuart, the road turns again to cross Indian River Lagoon onto Hutchinson Island. Here, Gilbert's Bar House of Refuge stands watch over a sandy stretch of coast. Built in 1876, the station was one of ten lifesaving stations commissioned along the Florida coast to provide assistance to and shelter shipwreck victims. The crew that lived, trained, and worked here had numerous opportuni-ties for heroism, including in 1886, when the brigantine *J. H. Lane* wrecked just five miles south of the station. Seven of the ship's eight crew members were rescued from the violently stormy seas.

Today, Gilbert's Bar House of Refuge is a museum. Inside, the rooms look much as they did when the lifesav-ers lived here. From its shady porch, you can look out to sea and let your mind wander back to the days when the now-busy island was a lonely strand of sand surrounded by vast emptiness and the men who lived here were the only hope for victims of sea disasters.

# 15

# CRACKERS and CASTLES

## MYAKKA RIVER STATE PARK TO ZOLFO SPRINGS

*Beginning at Myakka River State Park, head west on State Road 72 to Bee Ridge Road Extension, and turn north (right). After crossing Bee Ridge Road, continue onto Iona Road. Turn west (left) onto Palmer Boulevard and then north (right) onto Debrecen Road. At the intersection with State Road 780/Fruitville Road, turn east (right) for a short distance to Dog Kennel Road, then turn north (left). Continue with a slight right as the road name changes to Lorraine Road. At the intersection with State Road 64, turn east (right). Watch for the intersection with County Road 675/Waterbury Road on the right, and turn south (right) to the Rosa Fiorelli Winery on the right. Return to State Road 64 and continue east (right) to the intersection with County Road 665 and turn south (right). Turn east (left) onto Solomon Road and Solomon's Castle will be on the right. Return to County Road 665 and turn south (left), following County Road 665 as it turns east. Turn north (left) onto Hardee County 663 to the intersection with State Road 64, and turn east (right) and then watch for the left turn on to Wilbur C. King Boulevard. Once you've made this turn, you'll enter Zolfo Springs and turn into Zolfo Springs Pioneer Park.*

For all of Florida's spectacular natural spaces, the state has only one waterway that has been designated a National Wild and Scenic River—the Myakka. Over thirteen miles of this river are sheltered within Myakka River State Park, which, at fifty-eight square miles, is one of the largest of Florida's state parks. Together, the lazy winding river and the vast park with its prairies and wetlands make up a wilderness that is diverse, beautiful, and well worth exploring. Fortunately, it is easy to explore. There are miles of trails to hike; bike, tram, and airboat tours; and kayak and canoe rentals. The park is a birder's paradise and one of the best places in Florida to see lots and lots of alligators. Did we mention alligators? No, really: we mean a *lot* of alligators.

To the north and east of Myakka State Park lay vast tracks of agricultural and range land. Before the advent of air conditioning in the 1920s, much of Florida was inhabited by rugged pioneers, lawless brigands, and a tough-as-nails breed of pine-scrub cowboy that herded cattle with the crack of an eighteen-foot-long whip. These "crackers," as they were called, put the flat, mostly dry land to work as range land for the rugged cattle that were descended from hardy breeds brought to the area by the Spanish.

When the crackers herded their cattle to ports on the Gulf Coast, they followed a dusty trail that is now traced by Florida State Route SR 64. Today this road, officially dubbed the Cracker Highway, leads through the central heart of Florida.

Reminders of Florida's sub-tropical environment, such as this brightly flowering bromeliad, can be seen everywhere.

Moss-draped live oaks arch across a winding roadway in Myakka River State Park. Encompassing fifty-eight square miles of wilderness, Myakka River is one of the largest of Florida's State Parks.

Many large cattle ranches are still operating here, with vast expanses of green rangeland dotted by spreading oak trees. Citrus orchards, some of them extending for miles, are also a dominant feature in this area. Rosa Fiorelli Winery is a well-tended country gem. Fifteen years ago, Rosa and her husband Antonio moved here from Sicily. Finding the climate similar to home, they started a small vineyard and set aside space in the garage to make a few bottles of wine. Today, their three-thousand-square-foot state-of-the-art winery produces award-wining wines from the large, sweet muscadine and conquistador grapes that thrive here. Tours are available with prior arrangement, but visitors are always welcome to stop in their shop for a taste of any of their bottled varieties.

A few miles farther on the drive leads away from SR 64 through a countryside landscape of citrus orchards and small farms on the way to Solomon's Castle. In a state filled with wild and wonderful roadside attractions, few can match this one. The medieval-inspired structure was begun in 1972, when bearded and gnome-like Howard Solomon returned from a stint of living in the Bahamas, where he had developed a thriving following for his whimsical sculptures made from "found" objects. He wanted to build a studio to continue his work, but as he says, "I started building and didn't know when to stop." The result was a massive turreted castle surrounded by a moat containing an impressive sixty-foot-long, three-masted faux sailing ship that houses what Solomon calls with a smile "the best restaurant in Ona." It's also the only restaurant in town, but excellent nonetheless.

A tour of Solomon's Castle is well worth the price. Inside is an extensive gallery of Solomon's fun and quirky art, which can sell for up for five figures. The castle's shiny metallic exterior is the product of thousands of aluminum printing plates rescued from a local newspaper. Here, too, are fanciful one-person elevators powered by car batteries and starter motors, as well as eighty thematic stained-glass windows made by the multitalented Solomon.

Top: Morning sunlight and mist add an ethereal beauty to a view of the Myakka River, Florida's only designated "Wild and Scenic River." More than thirteen miles of the river are protected within Myakka River State Park.

Top left: This aluminum-clad castle near the tiny hamlet of Limestone is the whimsical creation of artist Howard Solomon. The castle is sheathed with thousands of aluminum plates collected from a nearby newspaper's printing press.

Top right: Solomon's Castle is filled with imaginative sculptures created by Solomon. Almost every sculpture has a humorous title or a joke or pun associated with it.

Moving on, County Road 663 leads through yet more eye-pleasing citrus orchards on the way back to the Cracker Highway, which heads into Zolfo Springs. Named for the sulfurous smell of its spring waters, Zolfo Springs has at least one attraction worthy of a stop. The Cracker Trail Museum in Pioneer Park features displays on the rough-and-rugged life of the early settlers.

Beyond the museum are half a dozen historic buildings that were moved here from around the area. Included are the C. A. Bryant Blacksmith Shop, a tiny rustic post office, and a rugged cracker frontier cabin. Zolfo Springs's Pioneer Park comes alive in late February and early March during Pioneer Days, when a huge contingent of re-enactors arrive to demonstrate the skills of frontier days gone by. The celebration is even better known for its antique tractor show, which brings up to four hundred exhibitors of antique diesel steam and gas engine enthusiasts together from all over North America.

If you arrive at any other time of year, you can still stroll along the banks of the black-water Peace River and imagine what it might have been like to chase lost cattle on horseback through this rugged landscape just one hundred years ago.

---

## 16

# The ROLLING CITRUS HILLS

### AVON PARK TO DUNDEE

*From Main Street in Avon Park, take State Route 17, which is at times marked 17A or Scenic Highway, north to US Highway 27. At the junction with Highway 27, follow Highway 27/State Route 17 north into Frostproof. Continue north on Route 17 into Lake Wales. In Lake Wales, turn east (right) on Burns Avenue for just over one mile, and then turn left into historic Bok Tower Gardens. End the drive here, or return to Route 17 and continue north to Dundee.*

Early in the twentieth century, Florida State Route 17 was the main north–south road through this lovely region. Built in 1918, the narrow brick road was designed to support the developing citrus industry and to encourage tourism traffic. To that latter end, it was named simply "Scenic Highway." Today it has been widened and paved but is still true to its name, traveling through a verdant landscape of rolling hills blanketed with deep green groves of orange trees separated by clear blue lakes. Farmers discovered early on that the soil here drained well and that the height of the land offered protection from the occasional frosts—making these hills particularly favorable for growing Valencia oranges. The first vehicles to use the road were probably farm trucks carrying ripe oranges to the juice plants. Tourists came later as they discovered the pastoral beauty of the region.

Avon Park is one of those central Florida towns that is easy to drive by without noticing, but the downtown here has two points of interest. The first, the Depot Restaurant, has been a legend in these parts for years, serving up heaping helpings of excellent home-cooked meals that keep every booth of the restaurant filled for breakfast and lunch (the deep, deep dish pies are highly recommended).

The other point of interest harks back to the days when Avon Park was trying hard to outshine neighboring Sebring. Investors trying to cash in on the Florida land boom of the 1920s chose to build the elegant Jacaranda Hotel here, and it filled an entire town block when it was completed. The hotel gained great media attention in 1926 and 1927 when the St. Louis Cardinals baseball team stayed there during spring training. It has also hosted such celebrities as Babe Ruth, George Burns, and Gracie Allen. During the Depression, the hotel's and the town's fortunes waned, but the hotel was recently completely renovated and once more offers upscale accommodations, casual dining, and a Sunday lunch buffet that is legendary among citrus country visitors.

North of Avon Park, the Scenic Highway veers away from the new US Highway 27 and once again curves through

Surrounded by lush gardens, Bok Tower is an Art Deco masterpiece that rises 205 feet atop a high hill just outside the town of Lake Wales.

Top left: **Boiled peanut stands like this one near Lake Wales are still a common sight in rural Florida.**

Top right: **The remarkable artwork on the brass door of the Bok Tower features thirty panels relating the biblical story of Genesis, starting with Adam and Eve being cast out of paradise.**

Bottom left: **Two sandhill cranes winter near Frostproof. About twenty-five thousand sandhill cranes migrate from Canada and the Midwest, arriving in central Florida in the late fall. The birds stand three to five feet tall and have wingspans of up to five feet.**

Bottom right: **It's harvest time, and a trailer full of oranges awaits transport to be made into orange juice.**

some picturesque citrus country. Sandy side roads branch in all directions, leading farther into the orange-tree-clad hills. Usually traveled only by locals and farm trucks, these are the perfect paths to take and follow your inner explorer. Scenic Highway continues through Frostproof, whose unusual name, according to legend, was not always popular.

It seems that as upscale northern settlers arrived, they didn't like the area's traditional pioneer name, used by the local cattlemen who knew that the range grasses here would not die out in the cold of winter. So the northerners decided to formally apply to change the town name to the more elegant Lakemont. Their mistake was in giving the application to an

# THE BOK TOWER

It's no accident that the two major features at the historic Bok Tower Gardens seem to mirror the personality of the man who created them, Edward Bok. The dramatic tower rising from the highest point of land could be said to represent the real world accomplishments of one of New York's hardest-driving and most successful editors, while the gardens represent the visionary and humanitarian goals that often were behind his great efforts.

Bok arrived in the United States at age six, the son of Dutch immigrants. He learned his entrepreneurial skills working in a bakery and later as an office boy for Western Union. By age twenty-one, he was running his own magazine, and by twenty-five he had been hired as editor of *Ladies Home Journal*. An innovator, he set aside the conventional wisdom on what women wanted to read, bringing in the era's most exciting writers who covered the popular topics of the day. As a result, the magazine was the first in the country to reach a circulation of one million, and it grew to be one of the major political forces of that time. He encouraged Helen Keller to write her autobiography, which was serialized in his magazine. He cultivated relationships with noted authors Mark Twain and Rudyard Kipling, and he even talked Teddy Roosevelt into writing a column under a pseudonym while he was still in the White House.

After thirty years as the magazine's editor, Bok retired to the land he had purchased near his beloved Lake Wales in Florida. Here, he set about creating what he originally thought would be a bird and wildlife

Bok Tower, designed by Milton B. Medary, rises 205 feet above Bok Tower Gardens.

sanctuary, but his efforts gradually morphed into spectacular gardens. Bok hired none other than the legendary Frederick Law Olmsted, garden architect of New York's Central Park, to design "a place of beauty second to none in the country." To anchor the gardens, he wanted a dramatic architectural structure, and with the help of Philadelphia architect Milton B. Medary, he created the plans for the Bok Tower. Construction began in 1927, and the finished tower was dedicated in 1929 by his friend Calvin Coolidge. Rising 205 feet above the hilltop, the elegant Gothic tower was constructed of pink and gray granite from Georgia and incorporated strong Art Deco influences, noticeable in the stylized herons that crown the building, as well as in the stone carvings and ornate grillwork that depict birds, plants, and wildlife.

The sixty-bell carillon was part of the tower's earliest plans, and today the facility keeps a skilled carillon player on staff who gives a performance each day at 1 and 3 p.m. Recordings of carillon performances are played throughout the day on the hour and half-hour. Bok lived just a year beyond the completion of the tower, but who knows: perhaps he still strolls through his gardens and gazes up at his beautiful tower with a smile of satisfaction.

Route 17 winds through rolling hills, past lakes and orange groves near Frostproof.

old pioneer to deliver on horseback. It seems that between "Lakemont" and the nearest post office, the name on the application was changed back to Frostproof, and Frostproof it has been ever since. Unfortunately, the name was not enough to prevent heavy frosts in the 1980s that devastated the local citrus industry. The industry has recovered, as evidenced by the healthy groves everywhere, including the orange grove that extends into downtown Frostproof.

At nearby Reedy Lake, you may get a glimpse of one or more pairs of sandhill cranes. Standing almost four feet tall, these magnificent birds wintered on the lakes in this part of Florida in the tens of thousands in the 1800s. But as the area developed and their habitat changed, the cranes almost disappeared. Then in the 1990s, thanks to conservation efforts, their numbers began slowly increasing.

This route continues through more orange groves before arriving in Lake Wales. Lake Wales's most famous destination is the historic Bok Tower Gardens, located just north of town. This must-see attraction offers the beauty of well-tended gardens and an exquisite 205-foot-tall pink granite Art Deco edifice known as the Bok Tower.

Edward Bok chose one of the highest points of land in the region to build the crowning achievement of his life. The visitor's center houses an excellent museum detailing the construction of the gardens and the tower. Winding through the gardens and around the hillside are a couple of miles of inviting trails. There is an excellent café here, whose peaceful patio is surrounded by gardens and offers a splendid place to relax. Or, you can purchase a box lunch for a picnic lunch and take it up to the oak-shaded lawn behind the tower. The upper floors of the tower house a magnificent carillon that is played hourly by a master carillon player. To sit here on a sunny afternoon—with the carillon bells sounding beautiful music and the lush green landscape of orange groves stretching to the horizon far below you—is an unforgettable experience and a sublime tribute to the visionary man who created this remarkable place.

# PART III

# NORTHEAST FLORIDA

A great egret displays breeding feathers in an attempt to attract a mate at St. Augustine's Alligator Farm on Anastasia Island. The profusion of alligators in the Alligator Farm provides the birds protection from predators, creating a perfect breeding ground for egrets, herons, woodstorks, and other large birds.

I F YOU ARE SEARCHING for Old Florida, it doesn't get any older than this. There is more history per square acre in this corner of the Sunshine State than in most places in the New World. It was here that the French established the settlement of La Caroline in 1563, and a year later that Pedro Menéndez established St. Augustine (after destroying La Caroline and murdering most of the French inhabitants). The beaches, rivers, and harbors of this coast are filled to overflowing with tales of murder, mayhem, intrigue, adventurers, and pirates. And then there are the ghosts. In St. Augustine, the headless spirit of the native warrior chief Osceola has purportedly been seen walking the battlements of the five-hundred-year-old Castillo de San Marcos. The nearby lighthouse has been declared so haunted that psychic investigators come from all over the world to experience its mysteries.

Spirits aside, there's plenty to recommend as you travel the area's backroads. Rivers and inlets form long waterways along the coast, creating immense expanses of wildlife-filled wetlands. This is home to Florida's longest river, the St. Johns, which is a favorite destination for anglers who come to test their skill against the bass and pan fish that lurk in its slow, dark waters. Along with the Tolomato, Matanzas, and Guana rivers, the St. Johns is part of Guana Tolamato National Estuarine Research Reserve, a sixty-thousand-acre preserve that protects vast tracts of north Florida's coastal estuaries.

South from St. Augustine, State Route A1A, otherwise known as Coastal Road A1A, passes the sparkling beaches of Anastasia Island and the historic Alligator Farm on its way to Fort Matanzas, which is a short boat ride across the Matanzas River. Farther south, the Ormond Beach Loop Drive links together oak-canopied, plantation-era roads. Not far away, the Old Brick Road—one of the few remaining stretches of "tourist" roads from Florida's 1920s era—leads for eleven miles through a remote corner of this region. To the north of Jacksonville lies the perfectly preserved eighteenth-century Kingsley Plantation, where a young and beautiful slave named Anna Madgigine Jai won her freedom and built a fortune of her own.

To the north are the broad and pristine sand beaches of Big Talbot and Little Talbot Island State Parks, whose beaches attract surf fishermen in droves and whose inlets and marshes are a favorite destination for kayakers.

All this is just a prelude to the fun and funky waterfront town of Fernandina Beach, which has been attracting visitors since the late 1800s. Here, too, is the magnificent Fort Clinch, whose cannon-topped brick ramparts still look out over Amelia Island's north shore. The fort is just another reminder that wherever you go along this quiet, laid-back coast, you're never far from human history that goes back a long, long time.

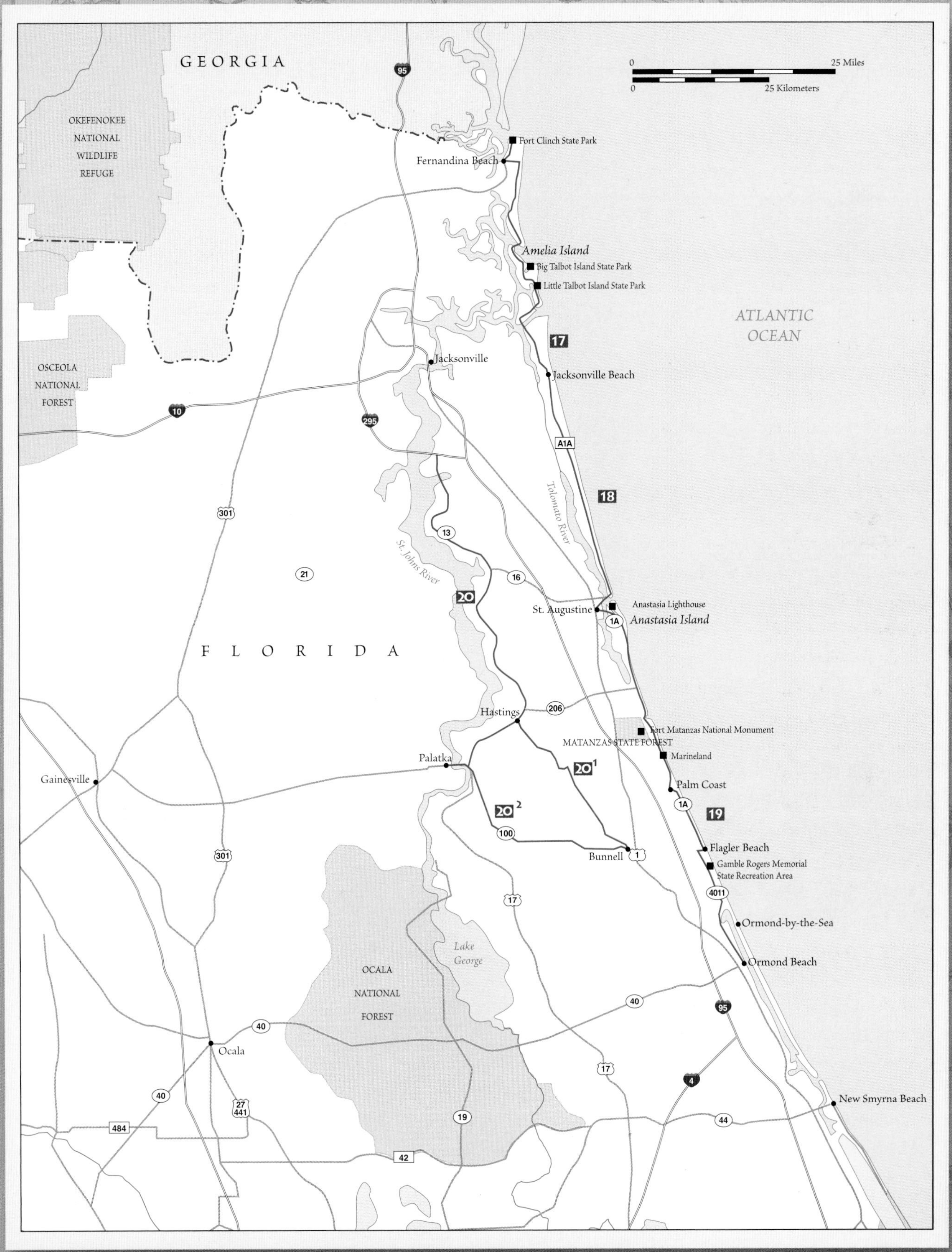

GEORGIA

OKEFENOKEE
NATIONAL
WILDLIFE
REFUGE

Fort Clinch State Park

Fernandina Beach

Amelia Island

Big Talbot Island State Park

Little Talbot Island State Park

ATLANTIC
OCEAN

OSCEOLA
NATIONAL
FOREST

Jacksonville

Jacksonville Beach

Tolomato River

St. Johns River

FLORIDA

St. Augustine

Anastasia Lighthouse

Anastasia Island

Hastings

Fort Matanzas National Monument

MATANZAS STATE FOREST

Marineland

Palatka

Palm Coast

Gainesville

Bunnell

Flagler Beach

Gamble Rogers Memorial
State Recreation Area

Lake
George

Ormond-by-the-Sea

Ormond Beach

OCALA
NATIONAL
FOREST

Ocala

New Smyrna Beach

0                              25 Miles
0                              25 Kilometers

# 17

# AMELIA ISLAND AMBLE

## JACKSONVILLE TO FERNANDINDA BEACH

*From Jacksonville Beach, drive north on State Route A1A to Mayport and cross the St. Johns River on the Mayport car ferry. Then continue north on Route A1A/State Route 105; watch for the sign to Kingsley Plantation and turn left. At the Y intersection, take the right-hand road, Fort George Road, to the Ribault Club. Continue on Fort George Road to Palmetto Avenue, and turn right to the entrance to Kinglsey Plantation. Return to Route A1A and continue north to Little and Big Talbot Island State Parks. Continue north on Route A1A, and turn west (left) on Atlantic Avenue and then north (right) on Fort Clinch Road into Fort Clinch State Park. Return to Atlantic Avenue and continue west into historic Fernandina Beach.*

The short ride across the St. Johns River on the Mayport Ferry gives you just enough time to step out of your car and admire the view. You might take a moment and picture how this river looked in 1814, when Zephaniah Kingsley arrived to establish a plantation on these shores. Kingsley was a believer in slavery, but he was also one of the South's most vocal advocates of humane treatment of slaves and preserving the rights of free blacks. In fact, Kingsley married one of his slaves, Anna Madgigine Jai, a Senegalese African whom he freed in 1811. She managed Kingsley Plantation and went on to own her own land and slaves, but their life changed for the worse after the United States acquired Florida in 1819. The new government repealed the more liberal Spanish laws dealing with free blacks and enacted harsh, restrictive laws. In 1837, the disgusted Kingsley moved his family to a new plantation in Haiti to protect them. Kingsley's house still stands on Fort George Island just north of the ferry landing, and it is open to the public. This is the oldest standing plantation house in Florida. The first sight that greets visitors is the ruins of twenty-five slave cottages arranged in a semi-circle. One of the cabins has been reconstructed to give visitors the idea of the primitive living conditions of slaves even on this "enlightened" plantation. Other buildings on the grounds include the elegant plantation house, the detached kitchen, and a barn.

A few miles from Kingsley Plantation stands a symbol of a more recent era of wealth. The Ribault Club took its name from the unfortunate leader of the Huguenots who was massacred, along with his followers, by Don Pedro Menéndez de Aviles, the founder of St. Augustine. The club was built as a resort in 1928 and was marketed to wealthy families in the North, who came to enjoy golf,

A banjo player performs outside a restaurant on Amelia Island.

yachting, and, as one guest put it, "the congeniality of a house party." The club faded into obscurity in the 1960s, but recently underwent a multimillion-dollar restoration and is now open to the public as part of the national park system. It is worth a short visit here to see how the wealthy

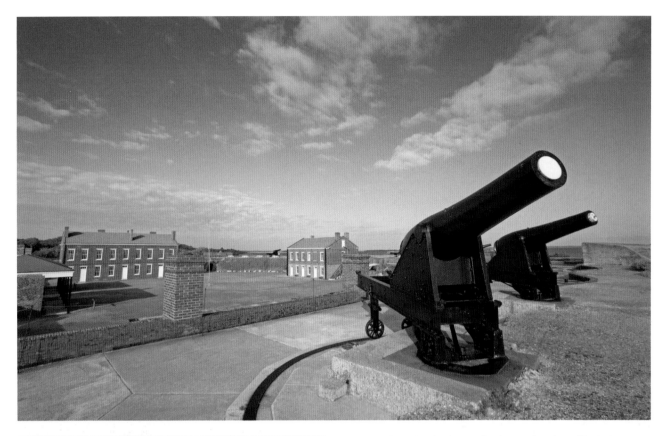

Above: **The unfinished Fort Clinch was abandoned by Union forces during the Civil War. Construction was never fully completed, although it was used for a time for coastal defense.**

Left: **A colorful collection of galleries, shops, and restaurants line the streets of historic Fernandina Beach.**

once played. The main clubhouse has displays that highlight Fort George Island's long and interesting history.

The coastline from Fort George Island to Fernandina Beach on Amelia Island's north shore is a nearly unbroken stretch of green wetlands and pristine shoreline, courtesy of seven of Florida's state parks. Big Talbot Island and Little Talbot Island State Parks are the largest of these, and between them they boast miles of some of the most unspoiled beaches in the state. The beaches of Big Talbot are slowly retreating, creating an ever-changing tangle of driftwood and gnarled, fallen trees along the shore that are a favorite subject of photographers. On Little Talbot Island, the broad, sandy shore appeals to anglers, as does the neighboring George Crady Bridge Fishing Pier State Park, where those fishing for red fish or speckled sea trout line the abandoned causeway and cast into the tidal inlet. Both Big and Little Talbot Island State Parks offer plenty of hiking trails that lead through the dense coastal forest

The Amelia Island Lighthouse, built in 1838, is the oldest lighthouse in Florida.

flag of these Amelia Island Patriots flew overhead. Then came the amazing adventurer and con artist, Gregor MacGregor, and for a few months his green cross flag flew aloft here. When MacGregor moved on, a pirate named Louis Aury moved in and claimed the island, flying the Republic of Mexico flag. The seventh flag was the Stars and Stripes, which flew after Spain ceded the territory to the United States in 1821. This was replaced by the flag of the Confederacy at the outbreak of the Civil War, but with the cessation of hostilities in 1865, the US flag flew once more. The Civil War also dramatically affected Fort Clinch. Construction on the large fort, which overlooks the entrance to Cumberland Sound, had been painfully slow since its inception in 1847. When war broke out in 1861, the fort walls were barely half way up, and the Union troops decided the fort was not defendable. They abandoned it, and the Confederate army occupied it for a time, but likewise decided it didn't have the resources to complete it.

Confederate soldiers built smaller batteries overlooking the entrance of the harbor but eventually retreated. The Union wasted no time in reoccupying the site and increased the pace of construction. Unfortunately, the types of bricks used for the beginning construction were no longer available, and the Union had to continue construction with larger, darker-colored bricks. Today, it's easy to trace the construction history of the fort as the buildings and outer walls have two distinct colors. The fort was never fully completed and was abandoned in 1869, although it was later occupied for short time during the Spanish American War.

Today, Fort Clinch is part of the state park system and is one of the best-preserved coastal forts from the mid-1800s. The buildings within the fort, including the officers' and enlisted barracks, a bakery, a mess, and a blacksmith shop, are still in excellent condition.

The fort's thick walls are riddled with long tunnels that lead to rooms with narrow slotted openings that once allowed soldiers to rake the moats with crossfire if they were attacked from land. Today, the ramparts are topped with large faux cannons (cleverly crafted from concrete) that give the fort an air of authenticity. The fort overlooks a long, pretty beach, and the park offers miles of hiking and biking trails and camping sites.

to remote sections of beach. Away from the beach, the low-lying landscape is crisscrossed by a maze of creeks and marshes that teem with birds and wildlife. These are a paradise for paddlers.

Just north of Big Talbot is Amelia Island, today a tranquil place, but it hasn't always been so. In fact, throughout history this little island has attracted a stellar cast of pirates, privateers, and adventurers, and it is the only place in the United States that has been under no fewer than eight flags. The French Huguenots and Spanish planted the first and second flags; the third flag belonged to the British. During the second Spanish occupation, the island was rife with smugglers, pirates, and slave traders. Fed-up locals with ties to the United States staged an uprising, taking the island and claiming Florida for America. The Spanish quickly took control again, but for one day the

As you exit the park, be sure to stop briefly at the Lighthouse Overlook, where a short trail leads to an excellent view of the Amelia Island Lighthouse. This lighthouse was originally built in 1820 on Little Cumberland Island. In 1839, however, the directors decided to move the lighthouse to Amelia Island, where it might be more useful. Having watched earlier lighthouses succumb to shifting shorelines, they decided to rebuild the light well inland on a high knoll of land and increase its height by fourteen feet so it could be seen from farther out to sea. Now the Amelia Island Lighthouse is the oldest operating lighthouse in Florida and continues to warn ships away from the shoals near the entrance of the harbor. In downtown Fernandina Beach, historic buildings with interesting one-of-a-kind shops and restaurants line the streets. The excellent Amelia Island Museum is a just a short walk from the main street and features an epic collection of artifacts and displays that relate the island's four-thousand-year history. A number of walking tours are offered through town, including a nighttime ghost tour that brings to life the stories of buccaneers, adventurers, and unique characters who shaped the history of this romantic and ancient coast.

The sand beaches of Big and Little Talbot Islands State Parks are so uncrowded that on some days you may feel like you have the park to yourself.

# 18

# ST. AUGUSTINE and the NORTH COAST

## JACKSONVILLE BEACH TO ST. AUGUSTINE

*From Jacksonville Beach, drive south on State Route A1A to Ponte Vedra Beach and continue south to Vilano Beach. Follow Route A1A as it turns inland (west) across the Vilano Beach Bridge and Vilano Causeway into St. Augustine. Turn south (left) at San Marco Avenue, which becomes S. Castillo Drive in the city's historic district.*

Driving through the elegant resort town of Ponte Vedra Beach today, it's hard to picture it as the hardscrabble frontier mining town it was in 1915. This was just a year after two chemical engineers discovered that the beach dunes contained a mother lode of minerals like rutile and titanium, which were crucial to the steel industry.

The settlement was purchased in 1916 by American Lead Company and named Mineral Town. The mines

A historic re-enactor uses hand bellows to heat up a forge in St. Augustine's Spanish Colonial Quarter. This living history museum recreates life in sixteenth-century St. Augustine, when the Spanish controlled Florida.

thrived during the height of World War I, when steel was in high demand, and as a result the company built a nine-hole golf course and a clubhouse, which were the precursor of the now world-famous Ponte Vedra Inn and Club.

During World War II, German submarines sank several ships just off Ponte Vedra Beach, and one dark night a submarine landed four English-speaking agents who carried large quantities of American dollars and explosives. The agents walked up the beach to Jacksonville and jumped on buses to other destinations. Fortunately, they were all captured before any of their plans came to fruition. After the war, mining slowed and eventually died out. Then the American Lead Company began developing this oceanfront tract as a first-class golf and beach resort. Today, golf is king in Ponte Vedra Beach, and the town is home to the Players Championship and the world headquarters of the PGA Tournament.

South of Ponte Vedra lies Guana Tolomato Matanzas National Estuarine Research Reserve, which protects almost ten miles of wild natural Atlantic beaches. It was here that some historians have suggested Ponce de Leon first came ashore in 1513 (although others have argued that it was St. Augustine or Melbourne Beach). If Ponce de Leon returned today, he might well recognize this stretch of shore, as little has changed here over the past five centuries. The reserve also includes great expanses of wetlands surrounding the Guana and Tolomato rivers. This large wetland is just a part of the expansive Guana Tolomato National Estuarine Research Reserve. All told, the reserve's seventy-three thousand acres includes vast tracts of wetlands along the St. Johns and Matanzas rivers, as well as ocean areas off the coast that are a calving ground for some of the four hundred endangered right whales remaining in the world today. The reserve's central feature is the new 6.2-million-dollar Environmental

The Castillo San Marco was built by the Spanish starting in 1672 to protect the town from attacks by pirates and the English. In the eighteenth century, residents of St. Augustine twice took refuge in this massive fortress as their town was attacked by British and colonial troops.

Education Complex that offers displays on the region's unique subtropical wetland ecology.

This route continues through Vilano Beach, once named for the villains who inhabited this sandy shore during Spanish rule. These days the town offers a small-town atmosphere and the closest beach to its more famous neighbor to the south, St. Augustine. The beach here is uncrowded, and cars are allowed on it. The Vilano Beach Pier is a great spot to watch the sunset.

Just across the Matanzas River is one of the most historic and fascinating towns in America: St. Augustine. Entire books have been written on its long and captivating history (see sidebar on page 103). With cobbled streets saturated in centuries of romantic underpinnings, this is a wonderfully walkable town. A good place to start your tour is along the inviting streets of the Spanish Quarter. The longest of these streets is St. George Street, where

the seventeenth- and eighteenth-century Spanish dwellings have been restored and are home to a dazzling array of shops, fine art galleries, and restaurants.

Similar but less-commercial streets branch in all directions, and if you stroll past the busy hubbub, you'll discover flower-draped, brick-paved streets lined by elegant historic homes and walled haciendas. Open gateways offer tantalizing glimpses into secret courtyards and gardens, and colorful flower baskets hang from second-story balconies decorated with ornate wrought iron.

You should definitely take a tour of the Castillo de San Marcos, whose walls twice sheltered residents when their town was attacked and sacked by marauding British-backed troops in the 1700s. Also worth a visit is the Oldest House on St. Francis Street, which dates to the early eighteenth century, and the Colonial Spanish Quarter—a living history museum with carefully reconstructed historic

Top: **St. Augustine welcomes visitors with an abundance of boutiques, antique shops, fine restaurants, and lovely flower-lined streets.**

Bottom left: **A horse-drawn carriage takes visitors past St. Augustine's oldest house. Built in the early 1700s, the house today is a historic museum.**

Bottom rights: **A historic reenactor portrays a sixteenth-century scribe in the Colonial Quarter of historic St. Augustine.**

## ST. AUGUSTINE: AMERICA'S OLDEST CITY

Following a long sea voyage in 1565, Pedro Menéndez first saw the Florida coast on August 28, the Feast Day of St. Augustine. Eleven days later, he landed and began to build a settlement, which he named St. Augustine in honor of the day he first spotted land. This was forty-two years before the founding of Jamestown and fifty-five years before the Pilgrims landed at Plymouth Rock. For the next two hundred years, the Spanish tenaciously held onto this settlement, but not without trial. After being attacked and sacked first by English privateer Sir Francis Drake in 1586, St. Augustine was attacked again in 1668 by pirate John Davis, who killed most of the townspeople. The Spanish responded by constructing the massive Castillo de San Marcos in 1672 to defend

Map of St. Augustine, 1589. *Courtesy of the Library of Congress*

the town. The citadel twice sheltered the residents from attacks: the first came from British settlers from South Carolina in 1702, and the second attack involved Georgians led by James Oglethorpe in 1740.

The British had control of Florida and St. Augustine from 1763 to 1783, ensuring that St. Augustine stayed Loyalist through the Revolutionary War. The Spanish regained control, though, only to sell the colony to the United States in 1821. St. Augustine's "golden era" began with the arrival of Standard Oil millionaire Henry Flagler in 1885. Flagler knew wealthy northerners longed for a warm wintertime resort that could be reached by train. He extended the rail lines south to St. Augustine and built beautiful hotels that today are some of the most graceful and recognizable buildings in the state. These include the Ponce de Leon Hotel (now Flagler College) and the Alcazar Hotel (now the Lightner Museum). He also built the city hall, a hospital, and several churches, including the magnificent, copper-domed Presbyterian church. Flagler ushered in an era of prosperity that continues today as visitors come from all corners of the globe to tour the historic streets and buildings of America's oldest continually inhabited city.

houses where period-costumed interpreters reenact the daily activities of early Spanish St. Augustine.

With so much turbulent history, it's not surprising that some of the most popular tours in St. Augustine are the evening ghost tours. Tour operators claim that St. Augustine is the third-most haunted city in the United States, after New Orleans and Savannah. Walking tours take visitors to old houses and cemeteries in the downtown area, highlighting such paranormal entities as the headless ghost who walks the parapet of the Castillo and the haunted parking lot where lights go on and off mysteriously. You should also take a stroll along King Street to see the

magnificent Ponce de Leon Hotel (now Flagler College) and the Alcazar Hotel (now the Lightner Museum). Both of these are spectacular Spanish Renaissance–style structures built by Henry Flagler during his development of the city as a tourist attraction in the 1880s. And by all means, every visit to St. Augustine should include a horse-drawn carriage ride. If possible, step aboard in the early evening when the lights of Anastasia Island send their enchanting reflections across the water, and the clip-clop of horses hooves on the cobbled streets makes it easy to believe that time has stood still in the oldest city in the United States.

# 19

# The PALM COAST

## ST. AUGUSTINE TO ORMAND BEACH

*From St. Augustine, drive across the Bridge of Lions on State Route 1A onto Anastasia Island and continue south on Route A1A. Turn left onto Red Cox Drive and follow it as it becomes Carver Street, and then turn right on Lighthouse Avenue to the St. Augustine Lighthouse and Museum. Return to Route A1A. The Alligator Farm is directly across the street. Continue south on Route A1A a very short distance, and turn left on Anastasia Park Road to Anastasia State Park and beach. Return to Route A1A and continue south to Fort Matanzas National Monument. Continue south on Route A1A to Marineland and then on to Washington Oaks Gardens State Park. Continue past Gamble Rogers Memorial State Recreation Area to Highbridge Road, and turn west (right). Then turn left on Walter Boardman Lane. Turn right on Old Dixie Highway, and make another right on Old Kings Road. Turn right again at the entrance road to Bulow Plantation Ruins Historic State Park. Return to Old Dixie Highway and take it south (left) to Tomoka State Park and continue into Ormand Beach.*

Question: how do you accidentally create a world-class rookery that becomes one of Florida's most popular bird-watching locations?

Answer: start with alligators—lots of them.

In the 1970s, the St. Augustine Alligator Farm was going through an identity change from a roadside curiosity to a first-class educational facility with the goal of teaching thousands of visitors a day about Florida's most intriguing wetland resident: the American alligator. The farm expanded its alligator swamp into previously unused acreage and a year or so later noticed a growing number of new springtime residents. Great egrets, roseate spoonbills, tricolored herons, and a dozen other bird species were building nests in the wetland trees. The reason why didn't take long to calculate. The alligators in the swamp below virtually guaranteed that tree-climbing predators, such as raccoons and snakes, were nonexistent. True, an occasional nestling that doesn't fly on the first try will feed the alligators, but overall, the Alligator Farm is the safest address around for raising young birds. It is also the best address for observing the birds up close, as the raised boardwalks that wind through the wetlands allow you to get within a few yards of the nesting birds, which pay no attention to bird-watchers. Of course, most people visit the Alligator Farm to see alligators, crocodiles, and animals from around the world. These include rare albino alligators; a 1,250-pound, fifteen-foot-long Australian saltwater crocodile named Maximo; and a host of exotic birds and mammals.

Heading out for a stroll on Hammock Beach near Marineland.

Left: A cannon still stands at the ready on the ramparts of Fort Matanzas. The small fort was built by the Spanish in the 1740s to prevent enemy ships from approaching St. Augustine along the Matanzas River.

Right: A perfect day for a drive along this palm-lined stretch of the scenic Ormond Beach Loop in northeast Florida.

Just a stone's throw outside the Alligator Farm stands the St. Augustine Lighthouse, one of the tallest and prettiest lighthouses on the Florida coast. Built in 1870, the 165-foot tower was constructed with more than 1.2 million bricks and boasts a first-order-magnitude fresnel (pronounced "fruh-NEL") lens. This elegant structure is both a working lighthouse and a historic museum. The lighthouse keeper's quarters contain several rooms of displays and artifacts that highlight the life and times of a lighthouse keeper, as well as the history of Amelia Island lighthouses (beginning with the wooden tower built on the island's northernmost shore in 1565).

If you enjoy a workout, you can climb the 219 steps that lead to the lighthouse's observation platform. On a clear day, this lofty perch offers panoramic views of the beaches and waterways of Anastasia Island as well as the elegant architecture of St. Augustine in the distance. And if you hear strange noises or feel a sudden chill while you're up there, don't worry; it's probably just one of the many lighthouse ghosts. The St. Augustine Lighthouse is purported to be one of the most haunted lighthouses in the United States, a claim that was supported when a television crew apparently caught an otherworldly specter on film. Other witnesses have reported hearing footsteps when no one was there or the crying of a child, which some say is the spirit of one of the three young girls who drowned in a freak accident during the building of the lighthouse.

If there is a site that deserves to be haunted, it is Fort Matanzas, as it was here that St. Augustine's founder, Don Pedro Menéndez, massacred more than one hundred French Huguenot soldiers who had surrendered to him. One hundred seventy-five years later, the Spanish, fearing an attack on St. Augustine through the "back door" of the Matanzas River, constructed this lonely stone tower where six soldiers and one officer lived for thirty days at a time. In its entire history, only one warning shot was ever fired from here, so the days in this remote fort must have passed slowly for the garrison. Today, the site is run by the US National Park Service, and with free admission it is one of the best historic destination deals in Florida. Visitors take a shuttle boat on a ten-minute cruise across the river to the fort. The meticulously restored fort is manned by a period-costumed interpreter who gives a short talk on the fort's history before turning visitors loose to explore on their own. The small structure includes the soldiers' quarters and the officers' quarters. If it is a sunny day, it's worthwhile climbing the ladder in the officers' quarters that leads through a narrow opening onto the roof. Here you can enjoy the sublime views up and down the river.

A short distance south of Fort Matanzas is Marineland, one of the country's first major oceanariums. For decades, this also was the biggest tourist attraction in Florida. Ironically, Marineland was not originally intended to be

Above left: **An organic vegetable vendor shows off a fresh handful of onions at the St. Augustine Farmer's Market.**

Above right: **The broad, well-packed sand of St. Augustine Beach is perfect for bicycling at the edge of the waves.**

Opposite: **An inviting gazebo overlooks a tropical landscape at Washington Oaks Gardens State Park.**

a public attraction. It was started as an underwater film studio conceived by an unusual partnership that included Cornelius Vanderbilt Whitney, a scion of two enormously wealthy families, and Ilya Tolstoy, grandson of famous Russian writer Leo Tolstoy. They built two huge tanks with a water delivery system that cycled five million gallons of seawater a day through them. The sides of the tanks had numerous windows that were to be used for filming. As the costs mounted, a suggestion was made to try to raise a little extra money by opening the facility to tourists who could watch the fish and dolphins through the windows. Imagine the partners' amazement on opening day, when the coastal highway was jammed for miles in both directions, as more than twenty thousand people came to see Marineland. For years, Marineland was the "it" place in Florida. Ernest Hemingway drank in the bar, and the restaurant was one of the best in the state. However, the opening of Disney World started a long period of decline for the attraction. The hurricanes of 1999 spelled the end for the original buildings, which had to be razed. In 2006, however, Marineland began a new chapter, building an impressive new 1.3-million-gallon pool system where visitors can have in-the-water interactions with dolphins. In 2011 Marineland became part of the Georgia Aquarium, and today offers many educational programs and opportunities to observe and interact with dolphins in the water.

In 1936, New York designer Louise Clarke bought a piece of land just a few miles south of Marineland that she and her third husband, Owen D. Young, retired to. Owen, in particular, was happy to be away from the pressures of New York City, where he had served as chairman of General Electric and was one of the founders of RCA. Here, along the Matanzas River, he and Louise planned and planted extensive gardens. Almost every day, a blue-jean-clad Owen could be found tending his citrus trees or selling his fruit at a roadside stand. Today, their lovely estate has been preserved as Washington Oaks Gardens State Park. The Atlantic beach here is unique, with fascinating coquina rock formations piled along the cinnamon-colored sand with tide pools at low tide.

State Route A1A continues south through the retro-looking coastal town of Flagler Beach. Sections of this highway run along the crest of an ancient dune rising high behind the beach, offering splendid views along the shore. The landscape changes drastically as you turn inland on Highbridge Road, leaving the bustling beach towns behind and entering a moss-draped world of marshes, woods, and waterways. A favorite day trip that locals have dubbed

Built in 1870, the beautiful St. Augustine Lighthouse is said to be the most haunted lighthouse in the United States. Visitors can climb 219 steps to the observation deck to enjoy a spectacular view of Anastasia Island.

the Ormond Beach Loop Drive, this series of charming, tree-canopied roads leads first west from Flagler Beach, then south along the old Dixie Highway, and then east on Granada Boulevard to Route A1A.

Dixie is an appropriate name, as this region feels more like the old South than coastal Florida. The landscape has changed little since the first plantation owners established cotton and cane plantations here in the late 1700s and early 1800s. In 1821, Major C. W. Bulow took possession of 4,675 acres of land in this area and cleared 2,000 acres with slave labor, establishing a prosperous plantation by growing rice, indigo, cotton, and sugar cane. Ten years later, several years after Bulow had died, his son was running the plantation when naturalist John James Audubon visited and described in a letter the new sugar-processing facility the Bulows were building. Five years later, the Bulows' genteel world came to a crashing

end during a Seminole uprising, when the plantation was attacked, looted, and burned.

Today, the ruins of the Bulows' sugar mill still stand in a sun-dappled clearing at Bulow Plantation Ruins Historic State Park. A path from here leads 6.8 miles through the woodlands that were once-productive fields to another clearing in Bulow Creek State Park, where the ancient Fairchild Oak spreads its massive branches. Estimated to be between five hundred and eight hundred years old, the Fairchild Oak is an outstanding example of the live oaks that once were a dominant part of the southern forests. This tree was already old when Audubon visited. And who knows: perhaps he sat here a time or two to sketch some of the egrets and herons, or the spoonbills, cranes, and wood storks, which in that not-too-distant past blackened the sky when they took flight in their astounding numbers.

# 20

# The MIGHTY ST. JOHNS RIVER

## FROM JACKSONVILLE TO PALATKA

*From Jacksonville, drive south on Florida State Highway 13/County Road 13 along the eastern shore of the St. Johns River to where Florida State Highway 207 joins County Road 13, and continue south. In the town of Hastings, turn left (south) and continue on County Road 13. CR 13 meanders southeast, and at the intersection with Florida State Highway 204, CR 13 becomes the narrow brick-paved historic Dixie Highway, "The Old Brick Road."*

*Option 1: You can choose to follow the narrow brick road for nine miles to the unincorporated community of Espanola (not recommended for low-clearance vehicles). At Florida State Highway 205, turn west (right), and follow Route 205 when it turns south (left) before intersecting with Florida State Highway 100/20 and then turn west (right). Continue northwest into the town of San Mateo, where the route merges with US Highway 17, and continue north and across the bridge over the St Johns River into Palatka. Turn south (left) on Moseley Avenue, and then turn east (left) on Twigg Street to the entrance into Ravine Gardens State Park.*

*Option 2: Return northwest on County Road 13 to the intersection with Florida State Highway 207 in Hastings. Turn southwest (left) and continue to County Road 207A and bear right, following Route 207A (stay to the right at the "Y" junction) to the intersection with East River Road and turn south (left). Turn south (left) on Putnam County Boulevard and then west (right) at the intersection with US Highway 17, and cross the St. Johns River into Palatka. Turn south (left) on Moseley Avenue and then turn east.*

A spectacular wildlife haven and fisherman's paradise, the tree-lined, black waters of the St. Johns form the longest river in the state and the second-longest north-flowing river in the US. It is also one of the laziest, dropping barely thirty feet in elevation as it travels 310 miles from its origins in the wetlands inland and north of Vero Beach to the Atlantic Ocean at Jacksonville. As the river approaches Jacksonville, it slowly widens into a tidal wetland that is often two or three miles across.

The St. Johns was formed during the last ice age as sea levels fell and sea water was trapped behind a barrier island. Later, as the land slowly rose, the water began gradually moving northward back to the sea. Today, the river and the sea remain in close contact, as the St. Johns is tidal for almost half its length, creating a rich habitat for a tremendous variety of wildlife. Twenty centuries ago, this wildlife included saber-tooth tigers and mastodons. Later, Timuacan Indians flourished here, and tens of thousands of them fished, hunted and built villages along the river's length. The Timuacan called the river Welaka or "River of Lakes." The first French Huguenot settlers called it Rivière du Mai or "May River." The Spanish had several names for it, including Rio des Corrientes ("River of Currents"), and Rio de San Juan.

Following an enticing trail on a late fall day at Ravine Gardens State Park in Palatka.

Left top: **A small sample of the many types of honey for sale at Bigger's Apiary roadside stand in San Mateo.**

Left bottom: **A wild azalea blooming in the woods of Ravine Gardens State Park.**

Right: **A collection of ceramic chickens on display at the unique Bigger's Apiary roadside stand. In addition to selling honey produced from their hives, they offer colorful pottery, lawn décor, Amish buggies, and a host of other fascinating items.**

*The Yearling* author Marjorie Kinnan Rawlings (see page 127) explored the river in a small boat in the 1930s. Impressed by the river's primitive splendor and dazzling wildlife, she wrote, "If I could have, to hold forever, one brief place of time and beauty, I might choose the night on the high lonely bank above the St. Johns River." Then, as now, the river is home to a tremendous array of wildlife. The waters teem with fish, manatees, blue crabs, and shrimp. Hawks and bald eagles build nests high in the trees along the shore. Deer and black bear haunt the forests; and foxes, raccoons, and river otters hunt along the river banks.

Today, CR 13 follows the eastern shore of the great river. Here and there, travelers can get a good view of the river lined with small, well-tended homes—many with long piers that extend into the black, tranquil waters, with all sizes and shapes of fishing boats and pleasure craft tied

alongside. A few miles after the road passes under I-295, a bridge across lovely Julington Creek marks the beginning of the seventeen-mile-long William Bartram Scenic and Historic Highway. The highway is named in honor of the famed naturalist and botanist William Bartram. Bartram spent nearly two years in this region from 1774 to 1776, researching and cataloguing the flora and fauna of the St. Johns and surrounding areas as part of his wider exploration of the US Southeast.

In Hastings, you will drive east for ten miles on CR 13 to visit the historic "Old Brick Road" (see sidebar). Here you must make a choice. You can drive this historic but bumpy lane (not suitable for low-clearance vehicles) for nine miles to the tiny hamlet of Espanola, and then head northeast along Highway 100. If you go this way you should definitely stop at the colorful roadside stand of Bigger's

## THE ROAD THAT TIME FORGOT

About ten miles southeast of Hastings on County Road 13, at the junction of State Road 204, a right turn leads onto a narrow lane made of brick that seems to disappear into a distant green tunnel of trees. Just nine feet wide and nine miles long, this seemingly deserted brick byway is all that remains of one of America's first interstate highways.

In 1914, the creators of the Lincoln Highway, America's first transcontinental highway, suggested the creation of a north–south route. This new route would allow the growing number of people who owned cars to drive from the Midwest to the tropical splendor of Florida. States quickly signed onto the project, eager to encourage the tourism and increased commerce the road would bring, but each state had its own idea of what the route should be. As a result, the Dixie Highway was not one road, but a network of paved routes with two major north–south arteries. Beginning just north of the Canadian border in Sault Ste. Marie, Ontario, one route led through Chicago and south through Nashville, Tennessee, and eventually to the gulf coast of Florida at Marco Island. The other route was more easterly, descending through Detroit; Asheville, North Carolina; and down the east coast to St. Augustine and Miami, terminating in Florida City. Several cross roads connected the two routes, allowing visitors numerous travel options.

When the Dixie Highway was completed in 1925, it was over five thousand miles long, and though called a highway, by today's standards it was barely a lane. The Ford Model Ts, Stanley Steamers, Chevy Roadsters and myriad other cars that traveled along it had to pull over on the wide shoulders to allow cars traveling in the other direction to pass. By 1920, many travelers were pulling lightweight metal travel trailers behind their cars, earning the road the nickname "Tin Can Alley."

The road had a relatively short life. As traffic increased, the need for wider, smoother highways doomed the original route. This section of the "Old Brick Road," as it is now called, is still minimally maintained and is drivable, though not recommended for low-clearance vehicles. Much of the original brick has been covered with a layer of sand, perhaps by nature, or in a man-made effort to protect it from the ravages of weather and traffic. If you decide to travel its length, you will find it leads through forest, ranch land, and wild backcountry to the town of Espanola. From here, you head to SR 100 and on to all the modern conveniences of Palatka, confident that you have traveled, for a short distance at least, through the pages of American history.

**The Old Brick Road near Espanola.**

Above: **A pretty park stretches along the riverfront of historic Palatka.**

Opposite: **The wooden bench at the end of this long pier is an open invitation to sit a while and contemplate the mysteries of the St. Johns River.**

Apiary where you can buy fresh honey, an authentic Amish buggy, a nine-foot-tall iron chicken, or any of hundreds of pieces of brightly colored Mexican pottery. Alternately, you can choose to return northwest along CR 13, then take SR 207 into Palatka.

In the mid-1800s Palatka was a small resort town and riverboat port where citrus and other goods were shipped to market. Today, the waterfront is still important and is home to a lovely park with pretty walking paths and a gazebo overlooking the river. The town's most prominent feature is a deep, water-carved ravine that leads to the river's edge. In 1933 at the height of the Great Depression, the workers of the Federal Works Progress Administration (WPA) helped transform this ravine into a stunning garden and park. They planted over ninety-five thousand azaleas, eleven thousand palm trees and 250,000 ornamental plants.

Today, the gardens are part of Ravine Gardens State Park and are one of the state's hidden treasures. A 1.8-mile paved road leads into the heart of the ravine and back, winding through verdant green landscapes and past brilliantly colorful gardens. The ravine road is open to cars but is particularly popular with cyclists and walkers. An easy hiking trail follows a small stream and features a hundred-foot-long swinging bridge across the ravine. The gardens themselves are most colorful from February to April, when the thousands of azaleas are in bloom. But anytime is a good time for wandering through this ancient geologic formation and marveling at the beautiful harmony that exists between the lush manmade gardens and the verdant natural landscapes of the ravine.

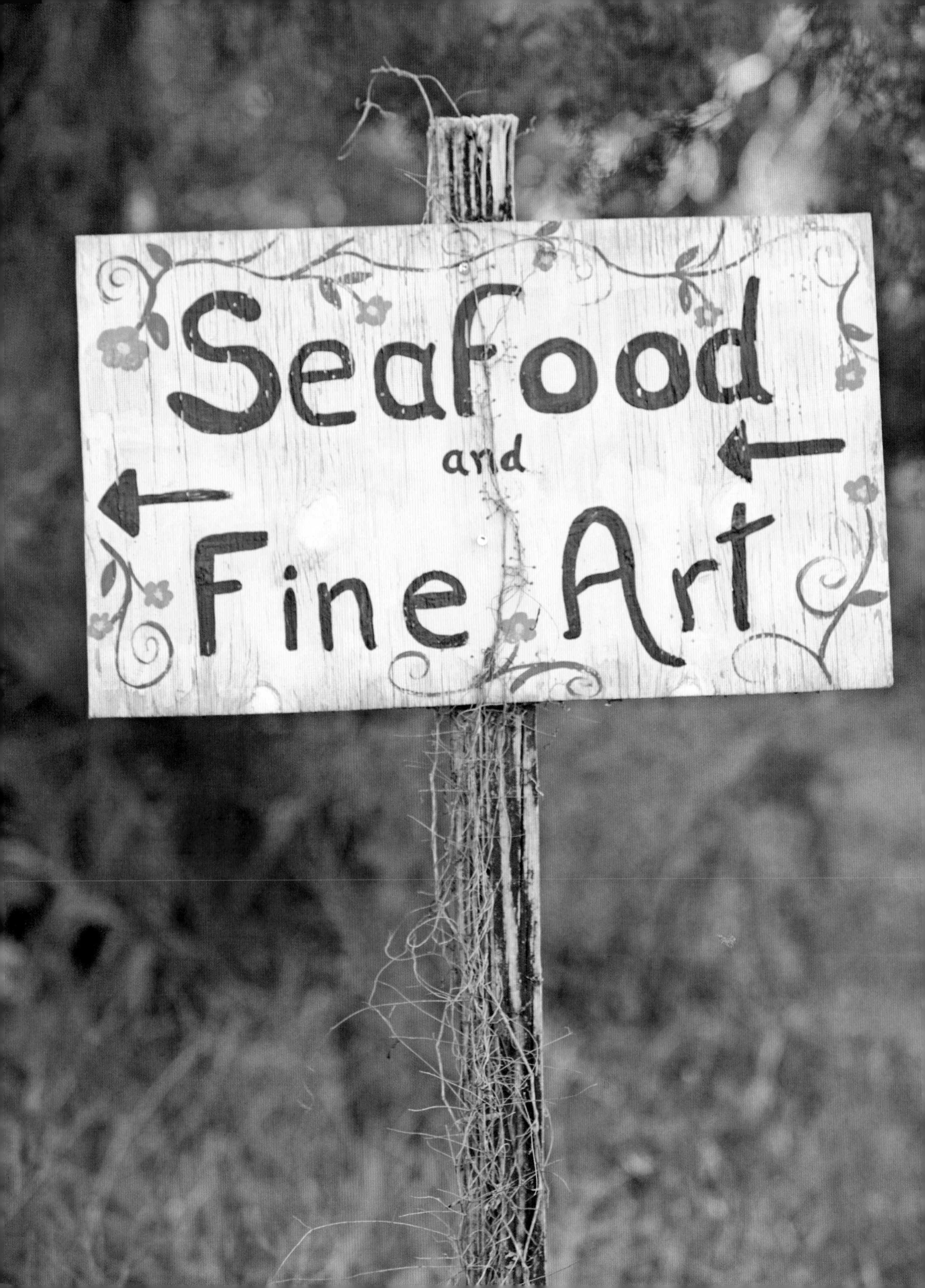
Seafood
and
Fine Art

# PART IV

# NORTH CENTRAL FLORIDA

A colorful, hand-painted sign advertises two of Cedar Key's most famous products: seafood and fine art.

I F THERE IS an area that breaks all of the sun-and-sand Florida stereotypes, it is the little-known north central region. Life here goes on at a gentle pace, largely ignoring the tourist hubbub of the other regions. The terrain is different, too. Vast cattle ranches blanket the landscape, creating panoramas of gently rolling grassy hills shaded by spreading oak trees. But if cattle is king, then horses are the rest of the royal family, particularly around Gainesville where immense equestrian spreads are bounded by labyrinths of white fences that look like they were painted just yesterday.

This area is pretty at any time of year, but it is especially beautiful in late March and April when wildflowers bloom abundantly along the roadways and in the meadowlands. Stables, barns, and one-mile racetracks are common sights along the backroads, as are gentle landscapes of meadows where you'll see plenty of graceful thoroughbreds grazing contentedly on emerald-green grass.

This is also blue spring country, and wherever you wander, you're never far from the sparkling turquoise splendor of these hidden gems of Florida. The state is home to more than 30 first-magnitude springs (springs that discharge at least one hundred cubic feet of water per second), and many of them are located in this region. The water from these springs has phenomenal clarity, having been refined for ages as it passes through the limestone bedrock to reach the surface. Many of these springs are surrounded with concrete walls to create more-or-less natural swimming pools that are very popular in the summer heat. But others, such as Ichetucknee and Madison Blue Springs, are still mostly natural, surrounded by cypress trees or jungle-like tropical growth that makes them breathtakingly gorgeous.

There are no real cities in north central Florida. Both quiet Ocala and the livelier college community of Gainesville ("Go 'Gators!") are really just overgrown small towns. Both offer all the needs of the modern world, as well as good restaurants. Even more fascinating are the unique and historic small towns such as Micanopy and White Springs, which look much like they may have a hundred years ago. The historic buildings along Micanopy's main street have been renovated into charming antique shops that attract a steady stream of visitors. Just a few miles away, the little crossroads settlement of Evanston is home to the Wood and Swink General Store, which has been in business since 1895 and houses the oldest continually operating post office in Florida.

Dubbed "the Nature Coast" by tourism officials, the region's two hundred or so miles of remarkable Gulf Coast shoreline are uniquely captivating. This isn't the place to come for sandy beaches. Here, there are no such sharp lines between land and water, as the low lying coastline seems to slowly melt into the sea, creating hundreds of square miles of magnificent salt marshes and wetlands that are home to an abundance of birds and wildlife.

Along this coast, you'll find the salty island community of Cedar Key and the historic fisherman's paradise of Steinhatchee, which together provide intrepid explorers access into the Suwanee National Wildlife Refuge, one of the most remote and splendid wilderness experiences left in Florida. Enjoy!

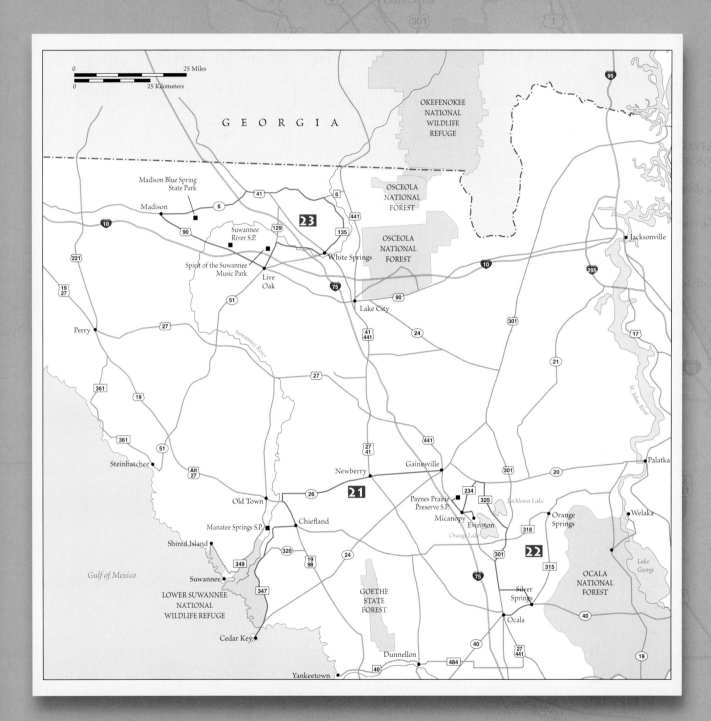

GEORGIA

OKEFENOKEE
NATIONAL
WILDLIFE
REFUGE

OSCEOLA
NATIONAL
FOREST

OSCEOLA
NATIONAL
FOREST

Madison Blue Spring
State Park

Madison

Suwannee
River S.P.

Spirit of the Suwannee
Music Park

Live
Oak

White Springs

Lake City

Jacksonville

Perry

Suwannee River

Steinhatchee

Newberry

Gainesville

Palatka

Old Town

Paynes Prairie
Preserve S.P.

Lochloosa Lake

Welaka

Manatee Springs S.P.

Chiefland

Micanopy

Evinston

Orange
Springs

Shired Island

Orange Lake

Gulf of Mexico

Suwannee

LOWER SUWANNEE
NATIONAL
WILDLIFE REFUGE

GOETHE
STATE
FOREST

Silver
Springs

OCALA
NATIONAL
FOREST

Lake
George

Cedar Key

Ocala

Dunnellon

Yankeetown

0        25 Miles
0        25 Kilometers

# 21

# The RIVER ROAD to CEDAR KEY

## GAINESVILLE TO CEDAR KEY

*From Gainesville, take State Route 26 west to Dudley Farm Historic Site, just east of Newberry. Continue on Route 26 to the junction with US Highway 19/27A/98 and head south to Dakotah Vineyards, just north of Chiefland. Then take Florida State Route 320 west (right) to Manatee Springs State Park. Return along Route 320 out of the park, and turn south (right) onto NW 107th Terrace. Turn west (right) on NW 102nd Place and follow it to 127th Court and turn south (left) to NW 90th Street and turn west (right) and then south (left) on NW 130th Avenue, which becomes NW Camp Azalea Road.*

*Turn south (right) at the intersection with County Road 347/SW Creek 347 and take it to the Lower Suwannee River National Wildlife Refuge. Then turn right onto the Lower Suwannee Nature Drive, and continue for nine miles until it returns to County Road 347. Continue south to State Route 24, and turn west (right) into Cedar Key.*

The two tiny farm roads that intersect in front of the Dudley farmhouse once formed the busiest crossroads in the region. Here, the busy Old Gainesville Road met the Jonesville Road, offering a promising site for Phillip Benjamin Harvey Dudley to establish a farm in the years before the Civil War began. He cleared the land, felling the tall pine trees to build a log cabin. Over the next one hundred years, the farm grew steadily, becoming a family-owned community

Above: **The ruins of an old stilt house stand in the shallow waters near the rustic fishing village-turned-tourist-haven of Cedar Key.**

Opposite: **A horse grazes beside a wildflower-filled meadow at Dudley Historic Farm State Park in Newberry.**

## THE QUIRKY HISTORY OF CEDAR KEY

After the close of the Seminole Wars in 1842, the settlement of Florida by land-hungry American pioneers began in earnest. Cedar Key's location on the Gulf of Mexico made it a logical transshipment point for goods shipped down the Suwannee River from the plantations inland. The town was settled around 1840 on Asenta Otie Island, just offshore from the current location. The shipping port greatly expanded after one of Florida's earliest prominent citizens, David Levy Yulee, brought his lifelong dream of a cross-Florida railroad to fruition. The railroad began in Fernandina Beach on the Atlantic Coast and ended at Cedar Key on the Gulf Coast, and dramatically simplified the transport of goods from America's heartland down the Mississippi River to the Atlantic Coast. Now, ships departing from New Orleans could stop at Cedar Key to offload goods for rail transport to New York and Massachusetts, rather than carrying them on the long and hazardous route around Florida.

History has a way of just strolling into town in Cedar Key, such as the time in 1867 when a young naturalist arrived on the island and announced that he had walked to Cedar Key from Indianapolis in just seven weeks. The naturalist was the twenty-nine-year-old John Muir. While he was at Cedar Key, he contracted malaria, which forced him to stay on the island and convalesce. He spent much of this time exploring the keys in a small boat and studying the birds and natural environment. It was at Cedar Key that he first postulated the theory that "nature was valuable for its own sake." Two years after his death, his account of his adventure was published in the book, *A Thousand-Mile Walk to the Gulf.*

Cedar Key was named for the thick stands of cedar trees that originally covered this and many of the surrounding coastal islands. In the 1850s, two pencil companies, Eagle and Farber, set up factories here. They did not make pencils, but rather fine-sawed the cedar into pencil-sized square sticks that were shipped by the millions to factories on the East Coast, where they were turned into pencils.

As Cedar Key's prominence grew, it garnered the attention of tourists, who as early as the 1870s were visiting "wild" Florida in droves. Resort hotels were built and facilities constructed to handle this new industry.

Left: **A tobacco barn stands serenely below moss-draped oaks at Dudley Historic Farm State Park. With buildings dating to the 1880s, Dudley Farm is a living history museum that reflects over a century of Florida's agricultural past.**

Right: **This backyard workshop at the Dudley Historic Farm State Park includes a sharpening stone and tree-stump-mounted vise.**

Bird's-eye view of Cedar Key, Florida, 1884. *Courtesy of the Library of Congress*

By 1880, the town's population had grown to more than ten thousand, making it one of the largest cities in Florida and one of the largest ports on the Gulf of Mexico. By this time, however, most of the cedar trees had been felled, and the pencil and other lumber mills began to close.

Then, in 1896, a devastating hurricane destroyed much of the town. Later, a fire leveled much of the business district, and eventually the town was rebuilt in its current location. Cedar Key continued to thrive for a time as a shipping port for lumber, fish, oysters, and brooms manufactured from palm fronds. Eventually, the railroad was rerouted to a better harbor in a then-small village called Tampa, and with the passage of time, Cedar Key slowly reverted to a quiet fishing village.

that included a general store and a cane syrup processing facility, as well as barns, a canning shed, a smoke house, and all of the facilities that comprise a self-sufficient farm. A hundred years later, Myrtle Dudley, part of the third generation to work the land here, donated the farm to the state. Myrtle, like the two earlier Dudley generations, had never significantly updated the house or outbuildings, and as a result, the farm was an astounding time capsule of Florida's agricultural history. From the liniment compounds still on the shelves of the shuttered general store to the dishes and original furnishings in the 1880s farmhouse, the farmstead had changed little since the days when it was the busy hub of a large corn and sugar cane plantation.

Today, visitors to Dudley Historic Farm State Park can start at the visitor's center, where exhibits and displays highlight the development of Florida agriculture over 150 years. The farm is a complex of eighteen buildings that

includes an open-sided structure where the Dudleys and their neighbors crushed sugar cane and boiled down the syrup. The centerpiece of the estate is the weathered Georgian farmhouse that is completely furnished with furniture, appliances, dishes, and décor that represent all three generations of these hardy Florida pioneers.

North of the town of Chiefland stands a newer but equally fascinating agricultural enterprise—Dakotah Vineyards and Winery. The winery got its start in 1985 when Max Rittgers planted two hundred muscadine grape vines. By the next year, he was selling the grapes at a roadside stand he built by placing a board over two buckets. Today, the winery produces nine varieties of wine, and more than thirty varieties of the heat-tolerant muscadine grapes are grown in the vineyards. The muscadine grape can grow as big as a golf ball and produces a heavy, sweet juice that is excellent for making wines that range from

a slightly sweet blush to richly flavored dessert wines, such as port and cream sherry. At Dakotah, a full tasting includes samples from each of the winery's labels, starting with the dry wines and working to the sweeter ones. Once you have made your selections, you are welcome to sit on the deck overlooking the duck pond or tour the carefully trimmed and tended vineyards.

A short distance from the winery, Manatee Springs Park is home to Manatee Spring, which spews out more than one hundred million gallons of sparkling clear water every day. True to its name, Manatee Springs is a favorite winter haunt of the West Indian manatees that come to escape the cold waters of the Gulf and Suwannee River. They stay here until late spring. In summer, the park and the spring are a favorite with local families who come to picnic and swim in the crystal waters that flow from the spring and travel just a short distance before spilling into the Suwannee River.

One of the longest natural rivers in the South, the Suwannee flows out of the legendary Okefenokee Swamp

Lower Suwannee Nature Drive. This narrow but well-maintained shell road leads through wild and pristine pine forest and hardwood wetlands. Here and there, short spur roads lead to boat launches that offer views of the river and marshes. However, an even better view of this wetland reserve is along the Shell Mound Trail a few miles farther south. Here, a millennium ago, first the Archaic and later the Woodland people inhabited this site. The twenty-five-foot-high mound was created from shells discarded during six thousand years of habitation. A short trail leads to the summit of the mound, which offers a superb panoramic view of the tidal marshes and creeks that are home to an abundance of oysters and scallops, just as they were one thousand years ago.

Cedar Key, the rustic fishing town and historic seaport turned laid-back tourist town, is the largest community along this coast. The town is funky and fun, and it offers an excellent selection of galleries, boutiques, and restaurants (one of the best is a hole-in-the-wall called Tony's Seafood Restaurant on Second Street). The Cedar Key Museum State Park features collections of shells, Indian artifacts, and more, assembled by wealthy collector St. Clair Whitman. The collection is housed in Whitman's house, which has been restored to reflect island life in the 1920s. A second museum downtown is run by the historical society and highlights the island's long and interesting history (see sidebar on page 120). A lot of Cedar Key's personality comes from the fact that the town is, and has always been, a working fishing port. The shrimpers still head out at sunrise, and a growing aquaculture industry raises clams in the vast muddy shallows of the surrounding tidal marshes. The visitors who come to Cedar Key come to fish or to get close to nature. The island is a gateway to the hundreds of square miles of wild Gulf Coast, marshlands, wetlands, cypress swamps, and pine and palmetto forests that seem to stretch in all directions. You can fill your days collecting oysters and scallops, or kayaking and exploring the vast and untouched wetlands. Or just sit and enjoy the warm sea breezes that caress this remote and untamed stretch of the Gulf Coast.

in southern Georgia and curves lazily for 266 miles before melding with the Gulf of Mexico through a series of tidal marshes and wildlife-rich wetlands. The fifty-three-thousand-acre Lower Suwannee National Wildlife Refuge protects not only a host of bird and animal species but also a magnificent coastal wetland environment. Within this unique area, you'll find fresh and saltwater marshes, cypress swamps, oak hammocks, and upland pine forests.

As you head south on County Road 347, watch closely on your right for the north entrance to the nine-mile-long

## 22

# The ROAD to CROSS CREEK

## OCALA TO EVINSTON

*From Ocala, drive east on State Route 40 to Silver Springs, and then continue east on State Route 40 to State Route 326 and turn north (left). Continue on State Route 326 as it turns west. At the intersection with US Highway 301, turn north (right) to County Road 325. Follow Country Road 325 to Marjorie Kinnan Rawlings Historic State Park. Continue on County Road 325 to the junction with County Road 2082 and turn west (left). Turn south (left) on County Road 234 to the junction with US Highway 441/State Route 25, and turn north (right). Turn right into Paynes Prairie Preserve State Park. Return to Highway 441/Route 25 and return south (left) toward Micanopy. At the intersection with County Road 346 and NE Hunter Avenue, turn west into Micanopy on NE Hunter Avenue. Return to Highway 441/Route 25 and continue east across the highway on County Road 346; drive to County Road 225, where you will turn south (right) into Evinston.*

Anyone who fondly remembers the 1946 Gregory Peck movie *The Yearling* will feel right at home in this friendly and homey corner of Old Florida. After all, this was the backyard of *The Yearling* author Marjorie Kinnan Rawlings, and it has retained much of its backwoods charm and beauty.

Silver Springs is one of Florida's largest springs, consisting of a group of fresh water springs in the headwaters, coves, and along the edges of the Silver River. The stunning beauty of the springs and river have drawn visitors since the end of the Civil War. Ulysses S. Grant visited here in 1880, and Calvin Coolidge enjoyed the springs in 1920.

Above: **Antique shops line Cholokka Boulevard in charming and historic downtown Micanopy.**

Opposite: **Sunlight illuminates Spanish moss hanging from live oaks along a curve of State Route 234 near Micanopy.**

Above: A fresh vegetable display brightens up the interior of the historic Wood and Swink General Store, which has been in business since 1895.

Left: The historic Wood and Swink Store in Evinston, near Micanopy, houses the oldest continuously operating post office in Florida.

Glass-bottom boats were invented here in 1878, when one of the spring owners put a glass window in the floor of his rowboat so his passengers could have a fish-eye view of the spring's spectacular underwater realm. Today, you can head out on the river in a modern multi-passenger glass-bottom boat that affords an even better view of the fish, artifacts, and formations that lie below the surface.

In 2013, management of the beautiful 231-acre head-waters section of Silver Springs was added to the adjacent Silver River State Park, and the new Silver Springs State Park was formed. The old amusement park and animal exhibits have been removed and improvements have been made that enhance the natural beauty of the park. The glass-bottom boat tours remain very popular, and canoe and kayak rentals are available. There is a viewing deck above the spring, paved trails, and ornamental gardens. There are nature trails for hiking and biking that provide opportunities to see native birds and wildlife, including alligators, turtles, great blue herons, great egrets, and ibis.

You may also glimpse one of the resident rhesus monkeys that call this spring and river home. During the heyday of the 1920s, the captain of a riverboat released the monkeys on an island for the amusement of visitors. The monkeys had no problem swimming off the island and soon set up residence along the river banks, where they have lived happily ever after. For years, a rumor circulated that the monkeys had been released during the 1930s filming of a Tarzan movie. The rumor was false, but the spring's jungle-like setting and crystal-clear waters have made it a popular filming location for movies, including parts of six Johnny Weissmuller Tarzan films.

The road to Cross Creek follows a narrow spit of land between Orange Lake and Lochloosa Lake. The tiny

## MARJORIE KINNAN RAWLINGS AND CROSS CREEK

In 1928, Marjorie Kinnan Rawlings and her husband Charles were contacted by Charles's brothers, who lived in Island Grove, Florida. They had found the country farm that Marjorie and Charles were looking for. The Rawlings wanted a quiet place where Marjorie could write and a place where they could renew their shaky marriage. They bought the farm and settled in. Early on, Marjorie was charmed by the land and the local people and began writing about them. Her first novel was published in 1933, the same year her marriage ended, leaving Marjorie to manage the farm herself.

In 1938, she published her third novel, *The Yearling*, to critical acclaim. *The Yearling* made her a national celebrity, a fame that only increased when the book won a Pulitzer Prize in 1939. In 1941, she married again and moved her permanent home to St. Augustine, and later she acquired a beach house in nearby Crescent Beach. She continued to spend time at Cross Creek, and in 1942 she received more public and critical acclaim for her book *Cross Creek*, the story of her early years struggling on the farm. One of the hardest chapters in Rawlings's life came when one of her oldest and best friends in Cross Creek, Zelda Cason, sued Rawlings for describing her in the book as "an ageless spinster resembling an angry and efficient canary."

Marjorie Kinnan Rawlings, 1953.
*Courtesy of the Library of Congress*

The suit demanded $100,000, and although she finally won, Cason was awarded only one dollar.

Rawlings later split her time between her beach house and a new summer home in upstate New York. She often visited the new Marineland (then the largest attraction in Florida), where her husband managed the restaurant, and she sometimes shared cocktails with Ernest Hemingway and other Florida luminaries, and was also friends with poet Robert Frost and novelists Thomas Wolfe and F. Scott Fitzgerald. She was active in the Civil Rights movement. Although she returned only infrequently to Cross Creek, she never sold the property. Perhaps the reason can be found on a sign that graces the entrance to the farm (now a state park), which displays one of her most famous quotes: "I do not know how anyone can live without some small place of enchantment to turn to." Rawlings died of a cerebral hemorrhage in 1953.

settlement of Cross Creek takes its name from the short stream that connects the two bodies of water. It was here that Pulitzer Prize–winning author Rawlings bought a seventy-two-acre citrus farm with her husband Charles Rawlings in 1928. Today, her farm is the Marjorie Kinnan Rawlings Historic State Park. A period-costumed interpreter does most of the farmstead chores. She also offers exceptionally informative tours of the house, which is filled with Rawlings's furnishings and books. In front of the house, the country lane leads to the actual village of Cross Creek, which is almost as small as it was in Rawlings's time.

Beyond Cross Creek, the route follows the Old Florida Heritage Highway, a delightful loop of two-lane country roads that passes through cypress wetlands, forest, and small farms on the way through some of the most inviting countryside in the state. The loop will take you north to the tiny and ancient farm community of Rochelle before heading south again past Paynes Prairie Preserve State

A Coke sign along the roadside in Cross Creek. Cross Creek was the home of Pulitzer Prize–winning author Marjorie Kinnan Rawlings. She used the town as the setting for several of her novels, including her best-known work, *The Yearling*.

are so many good antique and collectible shops in the tiny downtown that Micanopy has often been voted the best antiquing destination in Florida. A short distance north of Micanopy is Paynes Prairie Preserve State Park. William Bartram called this unique biosphere "the Great Alachua Savannah," and he was fascinated by its vast, open expanse of grass ringed by forest and dotted with wetlands. Water flows into this prairie from several sources, but it all goes out through the Alachua Sink, a relatively small opening in the limestone bedrock through which the prairie drains. When the sink fills with debris and no longer drains, the plain slowly fills with water until it becomes a lake. When this last happened in 1871, the lake became deep enough for steam-powered riverboats to transport passengers, supplies, and lumber along the lake. Twenty years later, the debris-filled drain unclogged, and the lake drained within a week. It is this drain-and-fill cycle that keeps the plain a rich grass prairie. In the 1600s, this area was part of the largest cattle ranch in Spanish Florida. Today, visitors to the state park can walk the trails and climb an observation tower to view herds of wild horses and buffalo that graze on the grasses, as well as view the many birds that call the grassy wetland areas home.

Returning toward Micanopy, this route turns east and then south to the tiny settlement of Evinston. There is little in this tranquil group of houses to attract attention other than the weathered cedar frame building that houses the Wood and Swink General Store and the Evinston Post Office. The building was constructed by a Micanopy merchant in 1882 when the railroad came to town, and it became a post office in 1884, making it one of the oldest continually operating post offices in Florida. As peaceful as the town looks today, it was rowdy in the early pioneer days. In the early 1900s, a gunfight broke out between store owner John Hester and a father-and-son pair of farmers named Barron. Both Hester and the Barrons raised watermelons, and older residents have recalled that the argument may have been over who had the prettiest watermelon patch. In any event, when the smoke cleared, Hester had shot one man dead and wounded the other.

Hester left town in a hurry, and sometime thereafter the store was acquired by H. D. Wood, the first in a long succession of Woods to own it. Today, it is owned and operated by Fred Wood III and the general store has been

Park to Micanopy. Micanopy (pronounced "mi-can-OH-pee") has been a popular place to live for a long time. When Hernando de Soto passed through in 1539, he noted a prosperous-looking village of Timuacan Indians here. Famed naturalist William Bartram visited this area in 1775, when it was a Seminole village called Cuscowilla. Bartram's book on his journey extolled the beauty and richness of the area. It was a bestseller, and settlers seeking good land soon arrived, making the town one of the earliest pioneer-era settlements in Florida.

As you drive into Micanopy along NE Hunter Avenue, you enter a village that seems like it was frozen in time around the 1940s. Many of the town's once-bustling mercantile buildings, including Doctor Daily's Drug Store and the Mountain Gas Station, have been renovated and turned into antique shops. In fact, there restored to look much as it might have in H. D. Wood's day. Part store and part museum, the shelves are stocked with Cokes and candy, food, books, and art for sale, as well as phenomenal fresh produce from his garden. Also a museum, many not-for-sale store fixtures, antiques, and vintage merchandise date back to the nineteenth and twentieth centuries. And a steady string of local residents come in to check their mail, buy some lettuce or radishes, and share news of local interest, much as they have here for over one hundred years.

---

## 23

# SUWANNEE RIVER RAMBLE
### WHITE SPRINGS LOOP

*Begin at the Stephen Foster Folk Culture Center State Park in the town of White Springs on the Suwannee River. Exit the park on Stephen Foster Drive, and turn northwest (left) on Osceola Street/County Road 25A. After County road 25A crosses Interstate 75, it will end at a T intersection. Turn west (left) on County Road 132 and then turn south (left) onto US Highway 129 to Spirit of the Suwannee Music Park. After visiting the park, continue south on Highway 129 into Live Oak, and head northwest (right) on US Highway 90/County Road 10 to the intersection with Stagecoach Road/Highway 132, then turn north (right). Continue straight ahead on 201st Path when Stagecoach Road turns to the right. The entrance to the Suwannee River State Park is straight ahead.*

*After visiting the park, continue west on Highway 90 to State Route 6. There follow Route 6 west (left) into Madison. From Madison, return east (right) on Route 6 and continue to the right turn into Madison Blue Spring State Park. Continue on Route 6 to the intersection with County Road 135 and turn southeast (right) and follow County road 135 as it curves around to the southwest and enters White Springs.*

Left: **Wisteria hangs in purple abundance along the river in Suwanee River State Park.**

Right: **An antique store beckons in historic White Springs.**

Left: **A young fisherman tries his luck at Suwannee State Park near Lee.**

Right: **An elegant bed and breakfast hints at White Springs's past. In the 1800s, White Springs was a thriving resort that attracted thousands of northern visitors to swim in its celebrated healing springs.**

When legendary songwriter Stephen Foster penned the words "Way down upon de Swanee Ribber," he had never actually seen the Suwannee. That's a shame, because this laconic and lovely river winds its slow and deliberate way for 266 miles from Georgia's Okefenokee Swamp through northern Florida to the Gulf Coast near the island of Cedar Key. For much of its route, the slow waters move lazily between green banks lined with moss-draped oaks and pine and palmetto woodlands. In spring and summer, wild wisteria, dogwoods, and azaleas wash the riverbanks with a palette of colors.

The Suwannee is one of the longest wild rivers in the South, and it is nearly as pristine now as it was one hundred years ago. In the 1800s, riverboats frequented its waters, and many communities developed around the docks, where plantations loaded indigo, cotton, and other commodities for transport to world markets. Later, steam trains replaced the riverboats, and these towns drifted into obscurity.

The largest town was White Springs, where a bubbling spring spewed forth sulfur-rich waters that reportedly smelled awful but were revered by early natives for their healing powers. In 1835, the springs were part of a riverside sea cotton plantation owned by Bryant Sheffield and his wife, Elizabeth. Touting the health benefits of the spring waters, the Sheffields built a log enclosure around the spring and constructed a small hotel, creating one of Florida's earliest tourist attractions. The spring was later

## THE MUSIC OF STEPHEN FOSTER

In the mid-1800s, nearly every household in America had a piano, a banjo, or at least a harmonica. Also in almost every home, you could find sheet music by the era's preeminent songwriter, Stephen Foster. From his earliest days, Foster had shown an astounding ability to create memorable songs that could be easily played and had themes that touched a common chord among people. This last quality might explain why Foster's songs have remained popular for more than 150 years. Even today, many adults can sing at least a few lines of "Camptown Races," " Dreamer," "Oh! Susanna," "Jeanie with the Light Brown Hair," or "Old Folks at Home," the last of which starts with the line, "Way down upon the Swanee River."

Songwriting was a trial-and-error process for Foster. When he was working on the lyrics to "Old Folks at Home," he was at first stumped by the first line. He originally penned the title to be "Way Down Upon the Old Plantation" and was going to use that as the first line, as well. However, he felt that a river location might be more romantic. The only two-syllable southern river he knew of that flowed through plantation country was South Carolina's Pee Dee, but somehow "Way down upon the Pee Dee River" lacked a certain punch. As he worked at his brother's desk, his brother referred to an atlas and suggested Florida's Suwannee River. Foster dropped a syllable, writing it as Swanee to fit the tune, and the rest is history.

Critics have often decried Foster's use of southern black vernacular in his songs as racist (he penned the first line of "Old Folks" as "Way down upon de Swanee Ribber"), but Foster was a northerner with strong antislavery feelings. "Old Folks at Home" is one of several songs he wrote in the voice of a homesick or world-weary southern African American. Many music historians believe that this was his attempt to introduce the idea that people from all walks of life share the same longings and emotions.

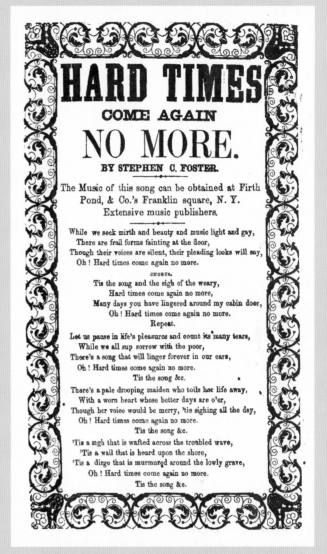

"Hard Times Come Again No More" by Stephen C. Foster.
*Courtesy of the Library of Congress*

As America's first successful full-time songwriter, Foster was also striving to write songs that would be sung both in parlors throughout the country and on the enormously popular minstrel stage.

Foster signed his first contract for sheet music in 1850. Over the next fourteen years, his fortunes rose and fell. He died penniless in 1864 at the relatively young age of thirty-seven, leaving behind a legacy of memorable songs that have delighted audiences ever since.

enclosed within a four-story building, with private therapy rooms and balconies where people could sit and watch the bathers below. Teddy Roosevelt took the waters here, as did Henry Ford. At its height, the town was so popular that it boasted fourteen large hotels. Today, White Springs's historic downtown includes more than eighty homes and buildings from that period, including a gazebo pavilion built atop the original foundations of the spring house, the Adams Brothers General Store (founded in 1865), and several churches. The town's side streets are lined with elegant Victorian homes and cottages once occupied by visitors who came every season.

Today, White Springs is best known as the home of the Stephen Foster Folk Culture Center State Park. Built in the 1950s, the visitor's center has the distinctive white pillars of an antebellum plantation.

Inside are displays and memorabilia from the songwriter's life. There are also two large paintings of Foster by renowned American painter Howard Chandler Christy. One depicts Foster sitting at his favorite writing desk surrounded by scenes from several of his most popular songs. The other depicts Foster in an idyllic Suwannee River setting. The highlight of the museum is the eight glass-enclosed cases that contain dioramas of scenes inspired by Foster's songs. Created in the 1950s by a local Florida company, these dioramas feature richly painted landscapes and figures carved with remarkable detail. Several dioramas feature small mechanical movements: fiddlers fiddle, people tap their feet, and there's even a tiny dog that wags its tail. Behind the visitor's center, a memorial tower rises two hundred feet above the surrounding gardens and grounds. The tower contains a ninety-six-bell carillon that regularly plays tunes from Foster's songbook and other music from that era. A small museum at the base of the carillon tower displays more Foster paraphernalia and two more mechanical dioramas.

Beyond the tower, paths lead through the beautiful grounds and along the banks of the black-water river that Foster made so famous. The river makes another appointment with music a few miles west of White Springs, where the Spirit of the Suwannee Music Park attracts top-named bluegrass and country musicians from all over the United States. This seven-hundred-acre riverfront facility includes a restaurant, campground, and

Two paddlers and a puppy head downstream on the Suwanee River near Dowling.

equestrian facilities, making it almost a city in itself on busy event weekends. If you want a good place to sit and watch the river, you can visit Suwannee River State Park, a low-key park that offers a good fishing spot and picnic facilities that overlook the juncture of the Suwannee and Withlacoochee rivers. If you've always dreamed of sitting under a shade tree and lobbing a worm-baited hook and bobber into lazy, dark waters full of bass and catfish, this is the place to do it.

Madison is an inland Florida town that is loaded with interesting historic buildings, but it has never been developed as a tourist destination. Sea Island cotton was king here in the late 1800s, when the Florida Manufacturing Company ginned up to ten thousand bales of cotton each year. One of the town's most impressive buildings is the Wardlaw-Smith-Goza house, designed in 1860 by Maryland architect William Archer Hammerly for prominent local citizen Benjamin Wardlaw. The house is now owned by the North Florida Community College and is considered a premier example of the classic Greek Revival architecture that is synonymous with the antebellum south.

A few miles east of Madison is Madison Blue Spring State Park. Although the spring is not one of the largest of Florida's blue springs, it is nonetheless a stunning oval of brilliant blue water about one hundred feet across, with access stairs on one end and an overlook on the other. The spring-head is deep here, emerging from a series of underwater caves that is a popular destination for certified divers. On hot summer days, this is a bustling swimming spot with families enjoying picnics and paddlers and tubers gliding along the clear waters that flow from the spring-head toward the Withlacoochee River. On weekdays, however, it is less crowded, and you can sometimes have the place to yourself. It's a good spot to enjoy the quiet beauty of nature before heading out along the gentle country roads that follow the north side of the Suwannee River through lush rolling farmland, where horses graze placidly and echoes of the Old South still can be heard.

In springtime, the fields and meadows of northern Florida explode in colorful carpets of wildflowers.

# PART V
# THE PANHANDLE

Miller's Landing Road is one of the green and shady historic canopy roads near Tallahassee.

Florida's extraordinary Panhandle region has been called the best of old-time Florida and the greatest repository of unspoiled Floridian wilderness. No need to choose between those descriptions, because the Panhandle serves up a stunning measure of each. To the early Spanish settlers, this narrow strip of land between the sea and the English colonies was of great strategic importance because it was home to the Old Spanish Trail. This rough trail connected St. Augustine, the capital of Spanish East Florida, to Pensacola, the capital of West Florida, and along it the Spanish built more than one hundred missions. More importantly, this road was part of the larger Spanish Trail, the legendary trade route that linked the east and west coasts of North America long before superhighways were imagined.

Today, much of the Panhandle is as wild and pristine as it was when the Spanish were here in the 1600s. Trackless pine forests blanket much of the upper panhandle, shading slow-moving black-water rivers that lure anglers and paddlers. Close to the Georgia border, the Panhandle has rolling hills that are home to cattle ranches and horse farms so green they look like they've been borrowed from Kentucky bluegrass country. Here you'll find the highest point in Florida, topping out at an "oxygen-starved" altitude of 345 feet above sea level.

This is not to say that all is backwoods in the Panhandle. Along the Gulf shore, some of the world's most beautiful white sand beaches have drawn a growing number of sophisticated travelers. Along the narrow ribbon of road known as Highway 30A, a dazzling collection of modern upscale towns have sprouted up. Built in the trendy New Urbanist style, they sport names like Watercolor and Rosemary Beach and offer houses starting in the million-dollar range. The nice thing about these new towns is that they share their riches. Visitors are welcome—even encouraged—to stroll the shop-lined streets or follow the boardwalks to the sugar-fine sands. And for those who want solitude, the Panhandle offers a series of breathtaking state parks along the coast. They preserve stretches of this wild and beautiful shore for the enjoyment of bird-watchers, beachcombers, and anyone who loves sea breezes, the soft sound of the surf, and the feel of sun-warmed sand between their toes.

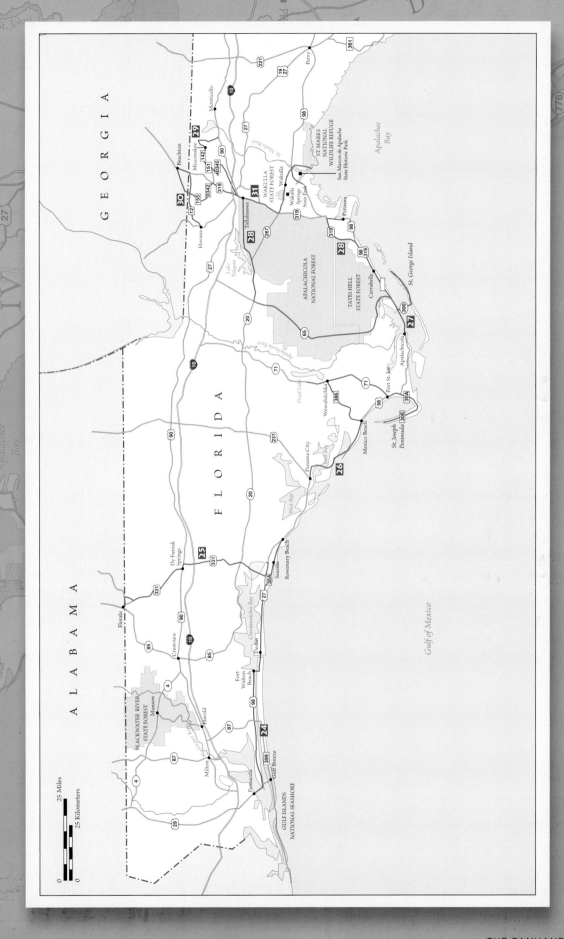

## 24

# ALONG the EMERALD COAST

## PENSACOLA TO ROSEMARY BEACH

*Start at Pensacola Lighthouse and Museum located on the grounds of Naval Air Station Pensacola, an active military base, where all visitors over sixteen years of age must show a valid photo identification and allow bags to be searched in order to enter the base. Drive east on Radford Boulevard a short distance to the National Naval Aviation Museum, then continue to Duncan Road/FL 295 and turn north (left), continuing straight as the name changes to S Navy Boulevard. At the intersection with Gulf Beach Highway/Warrington/FL 292, turn east (right). At the Y intersection bear left onto Barrancas Avenue, and then turn east (right) onto W Main Street. Turn north (left) onto Palafox Street and park near the next intersection, which is Zarragossa Street. Return south to W Main Street and turn east (left). Continue on as the street becomes Bayfront Parkway, and as US Highway 98 joins with Bayfront Parkway and passes the Pensacola Welcome Center (turn left at N 17th Avenue and then right on E Gregory Street to stop at the center). Continue south on US 98/Bayfront Parkway/Gulf Breeze Parkway across Pensacola Bay into Gulf Breeze. Bear right onto County Highway 399 toward Pensacola Beach and Fort Pickens. Turn west (right) onto Fort Pickens Road, and continue to Fort Pickens. Return on Fort Pickens Road, and turn north (left) onto County Road 399 to the intersection with US 98/Gulf Breeze Parkway, and turn east (right). Continue into Fort Walton Beach.*

*From Fort Walton Beach, follow US Highway 98 along the coast through Destin. After passing Topsail Hill Preserve State Park, watch for a south (right) turn onto County Road 30A, which follows the coastline through several upscale beach communities until it reunites with Highway 98 beyond Seaside in Rosemary Beach.*

To reach the top of the Pensacola Lighthouse, you must climb 177 cast-iron steps and clamber through a small door onto a narrow balcony suspended high above the ground below. You will almost certainly be out of breath, but the effort is worth it. The view stretches forever in both directions along the coast, making it easy to see why the Spanish chose this doubly protected harbor in 1559 to be their first settlement in what is now America.

In the distance, the busy shipping port of Pensacola lies nestled into the back of the bay. Just across the inlet, the green swath of a narrow peninsula bisects the harbor, and beyond that is the long barrier of Santa Rosa island, which holds back the unpredictable force of the Gulf of Mexico with miles of dazzling white sand beaches.

Today the landscape is beguiling, but in the 1500s it was wild and so inhospitable that the Spanish abandoned their settlement shortly after founding it, leaving St. Augustine, founded in 1565, with the claim as the oldest continually European-inhabited town in America. The Spanish returned to Pensacola in 1696 and made

it the capital of western Florida. Since then, Pensacola has flown several flags, including colors for the French, the British, the Confederate States of America, and the United States.

A stone's throw from the lighthouse is the National Naval Aviation Museum, whose remarkable collection of historic planes is rivaled only by the Smithsonian National Air and Space Museum in Washington, D.C. The planes on display here represent over one hundred years of military-related flight and include biplanes, early seaplanes, and four of the distinctive, blue A-4 Skyhawks from the legendary precision flight team, the Blue Angels, who are stationed in Pensacola.

In downtown Pensacola, the city's newly restored historic district is a great place to walk around. A stroll up Palafox Street will take you past a variety of restaurants, boutiques, and galleries—some that sport ornate wrought-iron balconies that reflect the town's French history. Heading east on Zaragoza Street, you'll find the Historic Pensacola Village, which contains a dozen or more beautifully preserved homes that reflect Pensacola's long and diverse history. The oldest of these, the 1805 Julee Cottage, is a charming frame dwelling that was once owned by a free woman of color.

Opposite: **A brightly colored umbrella marks someone's claim to a swath of beautiful white sand beach near Seaside.**

Top: **An RV travels along the coastal road through Gulf Islands National Seashore.**

Below left: **The brilliant white sand of the Panhandle's beaches accentuates the luminous green of the water.**

Below right: **This elegant Victorian-style home is just one of several you can explore in Historic Pensacola Village.**

Nearby are several good places to stop for lunch or a cup of espresso before walking on to the harbor. Once seedy, the town's waterfront has been reborn, and now boasts the lovely William Bartram Memorial Park, a marina, visitor's center, and tree-shaded walkways with inviting benches that offer a view of the comings and goings in the harbor.

From Pensacola, the route leads across the harbor to the small town of Gulf Breeze, which gained renown for numerous UFO sightings in the 1990s. Many of the reported sightings were made by highly reputable citizens, some of whom photographed and videoed a wide range of spooky airborne phenomena. After a spectacular mass sighting in 1998, in which eleven witnesses claimed to have seen a group of spaceships hover over the bay and then slide into the water, the sightings mysteriously began to decrease. UFO enthusiasts from all over the world still visit Gulf Breeze, and some investigators have suggested that the unusual sky-borne objects might have originated from experimental aircraft programs at nearby Eglin Air Force Base.

Another causeway leads to Santa Rosa Island and a magnificent six-mile stretch of undeveloped beach and windswept dunes that is part of the Gulf Islands National Seashore. In its entirety, the National Seashore extends for over 125 miles along the Florida, Alabama, and Mississippi coasts, and includes isolated, sandy islands reachable only by boat. The Santa Rosa section is an accessible dream beach for those who like their seashore wild and untrammeled. On a sunny day, a long walk along the shore can take you into a magic world of powdery white sand, emerald-green sea, and blue sky. The shore is often littered with shells, including sand dollars, lightning whelks, lettered olives, and tiny pastel coquinas. Sandpipers and willets scurry along the shore, advancing and retreating with the waves, while overhead the salt air is the domain of gliding pelicans and the aerobatic mastery of tiny terns.

The road ends at the entrance of Pensacola Harbor and historic Fort Pickens. Built between 1829 and 1834 to defend the harbor, Fort Pickens was for two years the home and prison of the famous Apache chief, Geronimo. The fort was updated several times before being abandoned after World War II (see sidebar on page 143). From here you can retrace your steps along Santa Rosa Island and beyond, driving along the coast, which offers a seemingly endless curve of beaches and bay towns. Twenty years ago, this stretch of highway would have been called sleepy even on a busy day. In spite of growing development, this is still one of the less-populated stretches of Florida coast, boasting some of the world's finest beaches with ultra-white, sugar-fine sands and translucent, emerald-green waters. Here, too, are vibrant wetlands and charming small coastal villages, as well as the dazzlingly chic, New Urbanist communities of Seaside, Watercolor, and Rosemary Beach (and more being built every year).

The charming gazebos that decorate the beach at Seaside are a favorite place for beachgoers to gather and watch the sun go down.

In the midst of all this, the town of Fort Walton Beach is an oasis of retro charm. The main street has a small-town feel, lined with shops containing galleries, boutiques, and restaurants. Part of the town's nostalgic aura emanates from the colorful storefront of Buccaneer Gifts, where owner Jeff Ring has been renovating and selling antique Coke machines and Coca-Cola paraphernalia for more than twenty years. Ring counts celebrities and Coca-Cola executives among the many customers of his beautifully restored nickel Coke machines and old ice chests, some of which date to the early twentieth century. Just behind Buccaneer Gifts, the town's beautiful waterfront park offers shady benches that have splendid views out across the Intracoastal Waterway.

Fort Walton Beach's history goes way, way back. It was here between AD 800 and AD 1400 that the native Mound Builder culture built the largest mound ever found along a saltwater shore. Experts have estimated that the mound, which is 17 feet high and 223 feet long at the base, took more than half a million baskets of earth to create. It was probably topped by a temple that was used for both ceremonial and social occasions. Today, the mound is surrounded by a small park, accompanied by an impressive museum that highlights the twelve thousand years that native cultures lived in the upper Florida Panhandle.

As you leave Fort Walton Beach, stop for a while at the Gulfarium, the oldest continually operating marine show in the United States. By today's standards this is a smallish attraction, but the passionate staff and highly entertaining shows make it a great diversion for beach-weary families.

Billing itself as the "World's Luckiest Fishing Village," Destin is certainly the busiest. Its harbor is home to more than one hundred charter fishing boats that range from hundred-foot-long large-group fishing boats to sleek high-speed boats that rocket anglers to the legendary, fish-filled, one-hundred-fathom curve that lies closer to the shore here than anywhere else on this coast.

Five miles east of Destin, Topsail Preserve State Park is one of six beach-front state parks that extend down this shore like a string of white pearls. Topsail is the largest of

Historic Fort Pickens was both a prison and a home for the legendary Apache leader Geronimo for two years after his surrender in 1886.

## GERONIMO AT FORT PICKENS

On October 25, 1886, a heavily guarded train pulled into the Pensacola rail station. On board were several very special prisoners bound for Fort Pickens. They were Geronimo, chief of the Apaches, and fifteen of his warriors. Geronimo's fame began in 1858 when he returned from a journey into Mexico to find that Spanish soldiers had murdered his mother, wife, and three young children. Leading small fast-moving groups of skilled Apache guerrilla fighters, he began a campaign of raids against the Spanish in Mexico, and later against American settlers in Arizona and New Mexico. Over three decades, he gained renown for his daring raids and ability to elude his pursuers. In the end, he and thirty-eight warriors spent months eluding more than five thousand soldiers, which was half of the army in the West.

After his capture, Geronimo was sent to Fort Pickens and became an immediate tourist sensation, drawing large crowds until he was relocated to Alabama during a yellow fever outbreak in 1888.

In his later years, Geronimo was allowed great freedom to tour as an attraction with Wild West shows, and he even rode in President Roosevelt's inaugural parade in 1905. However, he was never allowed to return to his homeland. He died of pneumonia at Fort Dix in 1909.

Portrait of Geronimo, circa 1886.
*Courtesy of the Library of Congress*

these, featuring more than three miles of virgin shore, towering sand dunes, and three beautiful dune lakes that are popular with anglers. This is a great place to take a break and stroll along the shore, digging your toes into the sand, which, as is true everywhere along this coast, is sugar-white and warm.

Beyond Topsail Hill Preserve State Park, watch for a right turn onto State Route 30A. In many ways, this road leads to another world. In the 1960s and 1970s, just a few small, funky beach communities dotted this ten-mile-long stretch of coast. This all changed in 1982, when a developer named Robert Davis decided to build a vacation community on eighty acres that had been left to him by his grandfather. Davis drove all around the South looking at communities and houses that he found attractive and inviting. He envisioned a beach community like those of his youth, with porches and paths and a town center with a general store and ice cream parlor. Eventually, Davis teamed with two architects, Andrés Duany and Elizabeth Plater-Zyberk, who had cutting-edge ideas about designing towns with walkable neighborhoods. The result was the little community of Seaside, whose picture-perfect streets were made famous when it had a starring role as the ideal town in the Jim Carrey movie *The Truman Show*.

Somewhat a victim of its own success, many of Seaside's once-affordable cottages now fetch prices of $1 million or more. Nevertheless, the town is pretty, open and inviting. Anyone can park along the main street and walk the sidewalks and narrow roads lined with white picket fences, visit the shops that surround the town common, or walk one of the many paths that lead to the fine-sand beach, each passing through its own uniquely designed beach pavilion.

Seaside was just the first in a wave of new upscale beach communities along State Route 30A, which now also boasts the larger communities of Watercolor, Seascape, Seacrest, Watersound, Alys Beach and Rosemary Beach. This strip of roadway is pretty, partly because of the beautifully designed communities and partly because there are still small traditional beach towns and stretches of undeveloped shore here, such as the mile of Grayton Beach State Park that gives the feeling that a bit of Old Florida still lives here.

— ● — 25 — ● —

# ROLLING FARMLANDS and MOSSY OAKS

## EDEN GARDENS STATE PARK TO FLORALA, ALABAMA

*Beginning at the intersection of US Highway 98 and County Road 395, turn north on County Road 395 (Port Washington Road) and follow the signs to Eden Gardens State Park in Point Washington. Return to Highway 98, turn west (right), and travel a short distance to US Highway 331. Turn north (right) on Highway 331 and drive across Choctawhatchee Bay, then watch for the intersection with County Highway 3280/FL 394/FL 81 and turn northeast (right). Turn northwest at the sharp left turn onto Black Creek Boulevard, then continue to Florida State Highway 20 and turn east (right). At the intersection with Florida Highway 81 turn north (left) and follow the highway past where it intersects with Interstate 10. Turn northeast onto US Highway 90 for a short distance, and then turn southeast (right) onto Ponce de Leon Springs Road/County Highway 181A. The turn into Ponce de Lion State Park will be on the right. Return to US Highway 90 and turn west (left) into De Funiak Springs for a few blocks, and then turn south (right) on Seventh Street to enter the town's historic district. After touring De Funiak Springs, return westward on Highway 90, past the intersection with Highway 331 South to Highway 331 North and turn right. After several miles, turn right on County Route 285 and follow this road north to Lakewood County Park. Continue on County Route 285 to State Route 54, which is near the Florida and Alabama border. Turn west (left) on Route 54 and follow this road to where it reconnects with Highway 331. Follow Highway 331 south (left) into Florala.*

The loveliest antebellum plantation home on Choctawhatchee Bay (pronounced "chawk-ta-HATCH-ee") is not really from the antebellum era, nor was it ever really a plantation home. But still, it is historic, offering a captivating glimpse into the gracious lifestyle that a few enjoyed in this semitropical Eden before the close of the nineteenth century. Eden is, in fact, what wealthy lumberman William Henry Wesley called his beautiful home nestled on the shores of Tucker Bayou. In 1890, he chose to build a practical, two-story, Low Country–style home with deep, shady wraparound porches and large windows to enhance ventilation. The house was the centerpiece of his lumber mill and the surrounding small mill community. A long pier in front allowed the easy transfer of lumber to barges that moved it to ships waiting in deeper water off the coast.

In 1963, the house was bought by Lois Maxon, who elegantly redesigned the porches with large columns in the classic Greek Revival style, reminiscent of Southern antebellum plantation homes of the 1850s in order to create a magnificent showcase for her incredible collection of antiques and heirlooms. Just five years later, in 1968, she donated the property to the state, which created Eden Gardens State Park. Today, visitors can tour the house, which still contains many of Maxon's fine antiques. The

A cherub dances atop a fountain surrounded by flowers in Eden Gardens State Park.

After crossing the bay bridge, the route leaves busy US Highway 331 and heads inland through the peaceful Florida countryside to Ponce De Leon Springs State Park. Although no one believes that the famous explorer who discovered Florida in 1513 was ever here, perhaps if he had discovered this delightful spring he would have believed that he had found the fountain of youth. Today, the spring is popular with swimmers who enjoy the clear blue-green waters, 68°F water temperature, and the natural surroundings. The park also offers two self-guided nature trails through the lush hardwood forest.

To the west, the town of De Funiak Springs is so richly historic that you may come away wondering why it hasn't been "discovered." In fact, it was discovered in 1884 by the Chautauqua movement. Started in 1874 on Chautauqua Lake in New York, the Chautauqua movement believed in bringing quality educational and cultural programs—featuring top speakers, preachers, musical programs, and entertainment—to rural areas. As the popular movement spread, new centers were established, and it wasn't long before Chautauquans looked southward for a warm-weather location to establish a winter home. De Funiak Springs, with its beautiful round lake and railroad station, fit the bill perfectly, and before long the Chautauquans had built elegant cottages and Victorian homes, established a college, high school, and teachers' college, and created a wide range of educational programs here. Many of the best speakers and entertainers of the day took the stage at the Chautauquan Brotherhood Hall, whose white dome rises high above the lakeshore. The Chautauquans also started a library that is still in operation.

One of the early leaders of the De Funiak Chautauquans was Wallace Bruce, who served as US consul to Scotland for several years. During his journeys in Europe, Bruce collected an impressive array of swords and armor, including pieces dating to the era of the Crusades. Today, many of these antique weapons, including sabers, pike heads, and massive broad swords, adorn the walls of the De Funiak Springs Library, adding yet another quirky chapter to this unusual town. Another interesting stop is the immaculately maintained Victorian-style railroad station that contains a small regional museum. A shaded portico on the other side of the tracks is labeled "The Opinion Bench," and true to its name contains not one but several benches on which

ten acres of grounds that surround it are tranquil and inviting, with pathways that lead to four small gardens. But the central feature is the long, green lawn shaded by huge, centuries-old, moss-draped live oaks that stretch down to the mirror-like waters of the bayou.

US Highway 331 heads north from Eden Gardens State Park toward the Choctawhatchee Bay. Shortly before crossing the bay bridge, stop on your left to visit the colorfully rustic shop of Elmore the woodcarver. This eclectic collection of Indian carvings, painted mermaids, and wizards carved from logs is a classic example of the roadside attractions that were once popular all along Florida's country byways.

Continue north across the bay bridge and causeway. The causeway is a popular fishing spot, and anglers of all ages can often be seen along the shore with rods and cast nets.

Above: **Briton Hill, near Lakewood, is the highest point in the state. Its modest altitude of 345 feet above sea level makes it the lowest highpoint in any of the fifty states.**

Right: **Two horses ham it up for the camera along State Route 285 near Lakewood.**

Opposite: **This plantation-style house, built in 1890 by William Henry Wesley, is the centerpiece of Eden Gardens State Park.**

the senior men of the town sit and swap stories, ideas, and, of course, opinions.

The Chautauqua movement faded in the 1920s as radio and the automobile made the outside world more accessible to rural dwellers, and with the onset of the Great Depression. But the impact of the Chautauquans on Florida's education system continues to this day, and the town itself seems to be just waiting for some new cause to come and help fill the ornate cottages that stand three rows deep around the stunningly beautiful downtown lake.

From De Funiak Springs, US Highway 331 heads northward through a rolling landscape of rich green meadows, hay-bale-filled fields, and horse farms ringed with tidy white fences, where it is easier to believe that you are in Kentucky or Tennessee than in Florida. This is the hilliest part of the state. Near the Alabama border, a side road,

Above: **Early morning light filters through the branches of an ancient oak on the grounds of Eden Gardens State Park in Florida's Panhandle.**

Right: **Stepping through the door of the Big Little Store is like stepping into the past. Baby Boomers in particular will recognize candy, toys, kitchen items, and household goods from their childhood lining the shelves of this one-of-a-kind store.**

State Route 285, leads to Britton Hill (named for a long-time postmistress of nearby Lakewood), where large signs in Lakewood County Park declare this to be the highest point in Florida. But don't anticipate lightheadedness or nosebleeds on account of high altitude, as this lofty summit is just 345 feet above sea level, proving that Florida and not Kansas is the flattest state in America.

A few miles north, you will enter Florala, just across the state line in Alabama. This pretty town is worth a stop if only to walk the path that follows the shore of Lake Jackson through stands of tall cypress trees. This is part of Florala City Park, and although the park itself is in Alabama, half of this round and very popular fishing and boating lake is in Florida. As a result, this town is a gateway for an annual migration of Georgia and Alabama residents heading to the beaches of the Gulf on vacation, and it makes a good place to relax and enjoy a meal before returning to explore more backroads along Florida's Panhandle.

# 26

# HONEY, SAND, and SCALLOPS

## PANAMA CITY TO ST. JOSEPH PENINSULA STATE PARK

*From Panama City, head south on US Highway 98 across the DuPont Bridge and follow Highway 98 (Tyndall Parkway), through Tyndall Air Force Base and Mexico Beach to County Road 386. Turn north (left) on County Road 386, and follow it to State Route 71. There, turn north (left) on Route 71 into Wewahitchka.*

*In Wewahitchka, turn right on Lake Grove Road and go a short distance watching for the Tupelo Honey sign outside an older private residence. From there, return to Route 71 and head north to view Dead Lake. From there, turn around and return south on Route 71 to Port St. Joe. In Port St. Joe, turn south (left) on Highway 98 and bear south (right) on County Road 30A to Cape San Blas. There, turn west (right) on County Road 30E (Cape San Blas Road), and continue to St. Joseph Peninsula State Park.*

This route starts with a pretty green drive through the heart of Tyndall Air Force Base, which covers twenty-eight thousand acres of the peninsula and barrier islands surrounding Panama City Harbor. Named for World War I flying ace Frank B. Tyndall, the base was hastily built in 1941 to train young pilots and gunners at the start of US involvement in World War II. Today, the base trains F-22 and F-22A Raptor pilots, and if you are lucky you may see these amazing aircraft performing aerial acrobatics at low altitude above the beaches or just a few hundred feet above the treetops.

After seeing the high-rise bustle of coastal resort boom towns like Destin, it is refreshing to come across old-fashioned, family-style beach towns like Mexico Beach and its neighbor, St. Joe Beach. The major attraction here is the beach itself, miles of it, bounded by the Gulf's signature fine white sand.

St. Joseph Peninsula State Park offers some of the most beautiful and untrammeled stretches of sand and surf in the state.

Above: **Sport-fishing boats lie quietly dockside as dusk settles over the marina in St. Joe, Florida.**

Left: **A family explores the colorful galleries and boutiques in the quaint, historic town of St. Joe. St. Joe was a company town until the close of the St. Joe Paper Company. Beyond the town lie miles of spectacular and virtually undiscovered sand beaches.**

Opposite: **A fisherman makes a perfect cast toward the sunset in the waters near St. Joe.**

The boundary between the two beach towns is County Road 386, which also forms the county line and the dividing line between the central and eastern time zones. So as you make the turn onto it to head inland, make note that it is now an hour later. This route is a time warp of another type as well, taking you from the busy beach towns into the laid-back heart of Old Florida. If there is an epicenter for the making of tupelo honey, it would be the little town of Wewahitchka. Here, the Lanier family has tended hives around the neighboring wetlands for nearly a century. Many people claim that tupelo honey is the sweetest and most flavorful of all honeys. As the Laniers are quick to point out, it's not they, but the hardworking honeybees, that make tupelo honey—and to do it, the bees need the sweet nectar of tupelo trees, which are commonly found in and around cypress swamps. The Laniers work

An angler casts into the gentle surf at St. Joseph Peninsula State Park. The park's 2,516 acres include miles of white-sand beaches, striking dune formations, and a heavily forested interior.

hard, too, gathering the combs and spinning the honey out in their backyard manufacturing operation. It was the Laniers who taught actor Peter Fonda the fundamentals of tupelo honey production for his role in the acclaimed movie *Ulee's Gold*.

For the visitor, the fun is in stopping by the Lanier house to buy a jar or two of honey. If you happen to be there when they are processing the honey—usually in March and April—you can get a tour of their honey processing operation. Otherwise, you drive along Lake Forest Road until you spot the hand-carved sign for their business and turn into the drive and a yard filled to the brim with sheds and outbuildings. The jars of honey are on a table in the shade of the side porch. If no one is around, just leave the cash under one of the jars. This is Florida back country, and businesses still run this way. From the Laniers' home, you can continue along Lake Grove Road or return and head north on State Route 71; either way you will soon come to a spot where you can view the Dead Lakes. The lakes get their name from the hundreds of cypress stumps

that stand in the water, giving the lake a surreal feeling. The lakes were originally formed when a sandbar closed off the flow of the river, flooding a low-lying area and killing the trees as a new lake was formed. Today, there is a small dam that regulates the water level. The submerged stumps and knees of the cypress trees make a fabulous habitat for bass. State Route 71 leads back to the coast and the small waterfront town of Port St. Joe. In 1835, the first town on this site, called St. Joseph, was founded as a deep-water port for trade. Then, when the railroad arrived, the town quickly grew to become the largest city in Florida, leading it to be chosen as the site for Florida's first constitutional convention in 1838. The first lighthouse was built in 1839, and the town continued to prosper until the outbreak of Yellow Fever in 1841. Disaster struck again in 1844, when a hurricane destroyed the town.

In the early twentieth century, the town, now called Port St. Joe, was rebuilt to serve as a company town for the huge St. Joe Paper Mill. For almost a century, the town and the mill coexisted and little changed. Since the mill closed in 1998, however, ever-increasing numbers of visitors are discovering the charms of this small, friendly town and the unspoiled coast along San Blas Peninsula. The town's main street, Reid Avenue, is a half-mile-long walk with an array of antique and gift shops and welcoming cafes. The San Blas Lighthouse was moved into Port St. Joe in 2014 to protect it from coastal erosion, and now stands in George Core Park on the bay. Stop in the visitor's center next door for information on climbing to the top of the lighthouse to see spectacular views of the bay. The Port St. Joe marina is a great spot to watch the sunset and enjoy a meal of fresh Gulf seafood. On the south end of town, the Constitution Convention Museum State Park commemorates St. Joseph and the long and impressive history of this area.

Perhaps the best part of a visit to Port St. Joe is driving out the San Blas Peninsula. The road starts south of town and traces the bay side of the peninsula, where the wetlands teem with wading birds and, according to the locals, the world's sweetest scallops lurk in the shallows. The road turns again to pass small groups of beach houses, ending some nine miles farther at the St. Joseph Peninsula State Park. The park offers a campground and boat ramps that give access to the bay. However, the real magic is found along the seven miles of fine-sand beaches that are totally undeveloped and so lightly visited that even in summer a short walk can lead to your own private world of sand, sun, and surf.

---

**27**

# The FORGOTTEN COAST

## APALACHICOLA TO CARRABELLE

*From Apalachicola, head east on US Highway 98/U.S. Highway 319 to Eastpoint and follow State Route 300/County Road 300 south (right) across the causeway onto St. George Island. There, turn east (left) to St. George Island State Park. Return across the causeway to the mainland and continue east (right) on Highway 98 to Carrabelle.*

If legendary author Ernest Hemingway were alive today, he might well spurn modern, touristy Key West and instead choose to live in the rough-and-ready oystering town of Apalachicola. Indeed, few towns in the United States have romance of which Apalachicola literally has boatloads. The waterfront bristles with the poles and nets of shrimp trawlers. Here, too, are scores of oyster boats of every size and shape.

Apalachicola has a worldwide reputation for producing the largest, sweetest oysters in America. Locals will tell you that the reason is the remarkable waters of Apalachicola Bay, which, when mixed with the freshwater of the Apalachicola River, create the perfect salinity for happy, healthy, and abundant oysters. If you have any questions about the importance of oysters to the local economy, look for the fifty-foot-high mountain of oyster shells that towers above the town's commercial docks at the end of Market Street. Here, the empty shells from a

dozen local processing plants are collected and eventually taken by barge back out into the bay, where they are placed to create new oyster beds.

In addition to this "Olympus of Oysters," there are two attractions in this scenic, salty marina that offer insight into the vast complex of wildlife-filled wetlands, barrier islands, and marshes that surround Apalachicola. The first is the visitor's center of the St. Vincent National Wildlife Refuge, where you can peruse excellent displays that describe this fascinating ecosystem and its flora and fauna. The refuge itself encompasses thousands of acres of bayside wetlands that include the barrier island of St. Vincent, which can only be reached by a private boat tour that departs from Indian Pass.

At the other end of the marina is the Apalachicola National Estuarine Research Center operated by The National Oceanic and Atmospheric Administration (NOAA). This education and research center encourages visitors to explore the river's tidal wetlands. A boardwalk trail leads into the wetlands, but before you follow that, you may want to visit the modern center's exhibits and display tanks that let you get up close to many species of sea life that are a part of the river estuary and bay ecosystems.

Apalachicola is not all rough and ready; it has a well-developed genteel and civilized side, too. The vibrant downtown area is filled with historic homes and buildings, many of which have been turned into restaurants, inns, boutiques, art galleries and specialty shops. Worth a stop is Grady's Market, housed in the riverfront building that was the J. E. Grady chandlery and mercantile during the town's heyday as a cotton shipping port. Originally, the store occupied one of the town's cotton warehouses. The current building was built after a devastating fire destroyed much of the waterfront in 1900, and today it houses more than a dozen shops. When you are ready to try some of Apalachicola's famous seafood, numerous restaurants will accommodate your desires. Papa Joe's Oyster Bar on Market Street is popular with locals, while the Owl Café and Wine Room is more upscale. Or, visit Hole In The Wall Seafood for casual dining.

Sweet, plump oysters, fresh grouper, and Gulf shrimp are favorites in Apalachicola. Beer pairs well with fresh oysters, and Oyster City Brewing Company produces and serves craft beer downtown on Avenue D. On your way out of town, you can grab a memorable cup of coffee and some of the rich home-baked goods at Café con Leche or step next door to sample the incredibly rich, dark, handmade chocolates of the Apalachicola Chocolate Company. Leaving Apalachicola, US Highway 98 crosses a high bridge, then

Left: Apalachicola is famous for its sweet, plump oysters; some of the best can be found at Papa Joe's Oyster Bar.

Right: Shrimp boats wait patiently at the docks in downtown Apalachicola. Between the abundance found in the pristine waters of Apalachicola Bay and the Gulf of Mexico, the town is world-renowned for its seafood.

Above: **The clouds on a perfect afternoon are mirrored in the tranquil waters of Cash Bayou, along Route 65, near Carrabelle.**

Right: **A single set of footprints are the only sign of human presence on this lovely stretch of fine sand beach at St. Joseph Peninsula State Park.**

travels east along a narrow causeway that offers splendid views of the bay and the Gulf, before arriving in Eastport. The harbor in Eastport is a popular shelter for the small oystering boats that tongers use. Tongers stand on the deck of their boats as they float in shallow water and open and close the scissor-like poles of rake-and-basket tongs to collect oysters from the bottom.

Eastport is also where the long causeway to St. George Island connects to the mainland. St. George Island's long and fascinating history includes pirates, shipwrecks, castaways, ne'er-do-wells, and a host of odd characters. Being off the beaten path, the island has mostly remained a quiet community of family beach cottages, reminiscent of Florida beach towns from days gone by. The island's entire northern end is home to St. George Island State Park. Here, wild sea oats grow scattered along the rolling dunes that protect nine

miles of one of Florida's most superb beaches. The park's main road extends most of the way to the tip of the island, making much of the beach easily accessible. The beach is seldom crowded, so even on busy days it's easy to find an empty stretch of sand to call your own. The beach's out-of-the-way address also makes it a popular stopping spot for endangered female loggerhead turtles, which begin arriving around May 1 to dig nests in the sand and lay their eggs. Nighttime lights near the beach can confuse the turtles,

## APALACHICOLA: THE TOWN THAT COTTON BUILT AND OYSTERS SAVED

Fortune smiled on Apalachicola when the first steam-driven riverboat chugged up the Apalachicola River in 1828. The river reached deep inland to Columbia, Georgia, providing a liquid highway through the heart of the Deep South's cotton belt. Steamboats made transporting cotton to market faster and vastly easier than the old method of hand-poled barges. Once downriver, the cotton was stored in the warehouses that lined the Apalachicola waterfront.

There, it was pressed into bales and loaded onto "lighters" for transport to seagoing ships that waited in deep water off St. George Island. As cotton poured out of the fertile inland farms, Apalachicola's population grew—from 150 in 1822 to more than 2,000 in 1838. By the mid-1820s, it had become the third-largest port on the Gulf, after New Orleans and Mobile. Cotton was so important to the economy that the town was at first called Cotton Town. Later, it was named West Point and then became Apalachicola in 1839. Sadly, as trains replaced river transportation,

the railroads bypassed Apalachicola, and the town slipped into decline. In the late 1800s, Apalachicola's revival began as Greek immigrants arrived and started Florida's first sponge-diving operation. The sponge fishery thrived here until it was moved to Tarpon Springs early in the twentieth century.

While searching for a way to cool the rooms of yellow fever sufferers, one of the town's nineteenth-century residents, Dr. John Gorrie, invented a machine that cooled air. This machine was the precursor to modern air conditioning, and similar machines later created the ice that allowed Apalachicola to finally capitalize on its greatest asset: oysters. The bay produces some of the finest oysters in the United States, and with the availability of ice, and, later, modern canning factories, Apalachicola's oysters could be shipped by boat and rail to markets throughout the country. By the late 1800s, oyster- and shrimp-processing plants were booming here, and Apalachicola was once again thriving. Today,

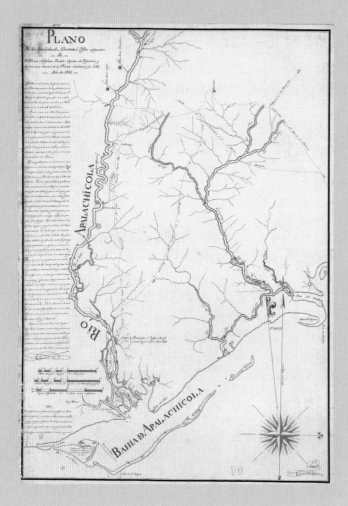

visitors will find evidence of the town's long history everywhere they look. Two of the town's original cotton warehouses still stand on Market Street, one of which houses the town hall. The Sponge Exchange building has changed little since the 1890s and can be found on E Street operating as an antique shop and sponge store. Here, you can purchase fresh sponges harvested from local waters by small commercial operations whose methods have changed little in a hundred years. A replica of Gorrie's magnificent cooling machine can be seen at the small John Gorrie Museum State Park on Sixth Street. Gorrie never lived to see the success of his system and would probably be amazed at the development of Florida, which the advent of air conditioning has made possible.

Map of the Apalachicola River, circa 1815.
*Courtesy of the Library of Congress*

who mistake them for moonlight reflections from the sea. As a result, the island residents, who are very pro-turtle, have adopted stringent lighting restrictions that give the island one of the darkest nighttime skies in the country.

Returning to the mainland, US Highway 98 traces the little-developed shore of Apalachicola Bay, creating one of the most scenic byways in the state. This is nature central: mullets jump, landing with a splash; wading birds hunt patiently for morsels in the shallows; skimmers glide inches above the mirror-like surface; and porpoises can often be seen feeding just offshore. Farther on, a bridge rises over the New River before descending into the little fishing village of Carrabelle. The protected harbor here makes it a favorite of sport anglers. Carrabelle is also home to the world's smallest police station. Actually, it's a phone booth. The story goes that for many years the local police

officers would park by this phone to take emergency calls and conduct business since they had no office. Today, their office is a not-much-bigger space in the town hall, and the booth is maintained as a low-cost, tongue-in-cheek promotion by the tourism department.

On a more serious note, Carrabelle is also home to the Camp Gordon Johnson Museum. During World War II, this section of the Florida coast was chosen to simulate the beaches at Normandy, and a base was quickly established to house soldiers who were being trained for the D-Day invasion. The museum has an extensive collection of artifacts from the base and World War II memorabilia. Most impressive, however, is the simple story of the scope of this massive effort, how quickly it was carried out, and the rough and primitive conditions that the troops had to endure during their training.

**Opposite:** A fisherman returns from checking his crab traps as dawn breaks over the calm waters of St. George Sound near Carrabelle, Florida.

# 28

# ANCIENT FORTS and SEA CREATURES

## TALLAHASSEE TO PANACEA

*Begin at Mission San Luis de Apalachee in Tallahassee, and then drive southwest on W Tennessee Street/US Highway 90 W. Turn south (left) onto Blountstown Street/State Route 20 West to State Route 65, and follow Route 65 south (left) through Apalachicola National Forest. Watch for signs to Fort Gadsden State Park, and turn west (right) on Brickyard Road to Fort Gadsden State Historic Site. Return to Route 65, and head south (right) to US Highway 98, then turn east (left) on Highway 98 toward Carrabelle. Continue on to the intersection with US Highway 319, and turn north (left) on Highway 319 into Sopchoppy. Continue on Highway 319 east to Highway 98, then turn south (right) into Panacea and continue south to Gulf Specimen Marine Laboratory.*

A few years back—say about four centuries ago—the Spanish settlement at St. Augustine needed more food than they could grow, and the Apalachee natives in the area that is now Tallahassee wanted a European settlement close by. The Spanish accomplished both goals by allowing two priests to start the mission that would become San Luis de

The Gulf Marine Specimen Laboratory and Aquarium in Panacea is a popular place for families, as kids love exploring the touch tanks, interactive exhibits, and other hands-on activities.

Apalachee in 1633. Eventually the mission grew to include a large chapel, meeting space, and military fortifications. The site housed not only religious activities but also hosted traders from Havana, St. Augustine, and elsewhere in the Spanish new world. Today, many of the original mission buildings have been reconstructed on the original site just two miles from the Tallahassee State House. Period costumed reenactors portray Spanish men and women, as well as Apalachee natives going about their daily tasks. This is the largest Spanish living history museum in Florida, offering a fascinating look at the complex interactions of cultures in the early days of European colonization.

Heading west from Tallahassee, the road through Apalachicola National Forest is green and captivating, but offers few distractions until you reach the turnoff for Fort Gadsden. And although it may seem like a long drive into remote country to see a historic site, Fort Gadsden should not be missed, as its strange history in many ways mirrors the political upheavals that forged Florida's early history. The site lies on a hauntingly peaceful bluff that offers spectacular views up and down the Apalachicola River. There is little here, other than some signage, to tell the fort's tragic story.

In 1814, the United States and England had been at war for two years. The British, wanting a base in Spanish Florida, sent Lieutenant Colonel Edward Nichols to build a fort and recruit Seminole natives and escaped black slaves to fight the Americans. He was also given a massive arsenal of muskets, cannons, and munitions. Ironically, just as Nichols was getting established, the War of 1812 ended. Nichols, however, longed to continue the fight, hoping to bring resolution to the issue of slavery and the plight of

disenfranchised Native Americans. Leaving to pursue a political resolution, he turned over the fort to the roughly 270 blacks and 30 Seminoles who remained, with orders to "defend the fort against any and all threats."

The fort, with its largely black contingent, had become a magnet for runaway Southern slaves. Not surprisingly, this infuriated Southern landholders who petitioned Washington to put an end to "The Negro Fort." The US government once again dispatched the "Hero of New Orleans," Andrew Jackson, who built his own fort on the Flint River just north of the Florida border, from which he launched an attack. The actual battle was remarkably brief. The Navy sent two ships upriver from the Gulf, and on their fifth exchange of fire with the fort, a heated cannonball went over the fort walls and landed in the massive munitions store. The resulting explosion killed 270 of the 300 men, women, and children inside the fort, and was heard a hundred miles away in Pensacola. Today, the gentle

Left: **A costumed interpreter portrays a well-to-do Spanish woman of the early 1700s at Mission San Luis in Tallahassee.**

Below: **One of the most remotely beautiful places in the Florida Panhandle, Fort Gadsden National Historic Site, overlooking the Apalachicola River, was the site of a tragic battle in 1816.**

breezes stirring the grassy banks of the river belie the carnage that occurred almost two hundred years ago.

Returning to State Route 65, this route continues for miles through pleasant green landscapes, the town of Carrabelle, and along the Gulf Coast, eventually reentering civilization at the funky little burg of Sopchoppy. This is an art town in-the-making with one or two gift shops and a recording studio. It's a good place to stop, drop in the little market for a soda, and walk around for a few minutes.

Farther along, Panacea is a larger, rambling town that sits at the edge of the vast St. Marks National Wildlife Refuge. Traditionally a fishing town, Panacea is perhaps best known as home to the Gulf Specimen Marine Laboratory and

Aquarium. This unique attraction should not be missed, particularly if there are children in your party. The lab is the brainchild of environmental activists, biologists, and authors Jack and Anne Rudloe. There are several buildings, each filled with saltwater tanks in which many common and not-so-common fish, shellfish, and other critters can be found. The lab is particularly popular with school groups, and kids can often be heard laughing and screaming in delight as they get to touch and see animals that they have only heard of. "One of my big goals is to get kids to touch these animals," Jack Rudloe said about establishing the aquarium. "If they touch them and hold them, they stop being afraid. Then curiosity sets in and the learning starts."

---

## 29

# A WANDER THROUGH YESTERYEAR

## TALLAHASSEE'S CANOPY ROADS

*In Tallahassee, start at the Goodwood Museum and Gardens. Take Miccosukee Road northeast to Crump Road and turn north (left). Go to Roberts Road and turn west (left) and go to Centerville Road (County Road 151) and turn northeast (right). Watch on your left for Pisgah Road, but turn right on the small unpaved road and go a short distance to Pisgah Church. Return to Centerville Road (County Road 151) and turn northeast (right). Watch on the right for Bradley's General Store. Continue on Centerville Road (County Road 151), which becomes Moccasin Gap Road (County Road 151) and enters the small settlement of Miccosukee at the intersection of Moccasin Gap and Miccosukee Roads. Continue on Moccasin Gap Road to TS Green Road and turn north (left). Continue to Magnolia Road (County Road 142) and turn south (right). Continue south along Magnolia Road to Mahan Drive (US Highway 90) and turn right toward Tallahassee. Immediately after the intersection with Interstate 10, take the first right into the Tallahassee Auto Museum, and then return to Mahan Drive/ US Highway 90 and continue west into Tallahassee.*

*Note: When Magnolia Road crosses Cromartie Road, the road becomes a narrow, graded dirt road. While this road is usually very drivable, wet weather can render it impassable to low-clearance cars. If you do not wish to attempt this part of the scenic route, you may return along Cromartie Road, which becomes Moccasin Gap Road and then Centerville Road (County Road 151). From Centerville Road, head back southwest toward Tallahassee.*

If Tallahassee has a signature feature, it is the shady, inviting two-lane roads that wind out of the city. These roads, lying beneath dense green canopies of oak, pecan, magnolia, and a dozen other species of trees, began as primitive paths through thick native forests. In the nineteenth century, as more land went under the plow, plantation owners were careful to maintain the tree borders along these old roads to shade travelers—including their own workers, who

drove mule wagons through here piled high with cotton— from the hot summer sun. Today, Tallahassee has carefully preserved seven of these historic canopy roads, which offer modern travelers a delightfully pastoral and scenic drive. This backroad outing will introduce you to two of the best: Centerville Road and Miccosukee Road.

Before you head out on these, however, you should take time to tour the place where Florida senator William C.

The red clay surface of Old Magnolia Road splits in two directions to go around the ancient live oak known as "The Dueling Oak." Shaded and inviting, the byway is one of Tallahassee's historic canopy roads.

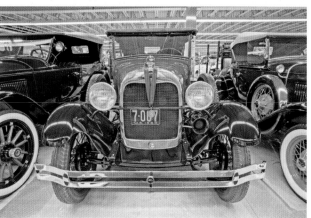

Top: **Famous for their handmade smoked sausage, Bradley's Country Store still provides locals with everyday goods just as it has for more than eighty years.**

Bottom left: **Trees stand in neat and orderly rows as far as the eye can see on this pine plantation north of Tallahassee.**

Bottom right: **A line of antique cars stands polished and ready to greet visitors at the Tallahassee Automobile Museum. The museum contains over 140 antique and classic cars, including three different Batmobiles from television and movie adaptations of the comic** *Batman.*

Hodges once joked that he bought the most expensive bed of his life. In the mid-1920s, his wife had been a frequent guest at the elegant Goodwood Plantation House just outside Tallahassee. She had admired one of the beds and asked her husband to buy it for her if possible. The plantation owner was not eager to part with the bed, which she felt belonged with the house; the house, however, was for sale. In the end, the only way the senator could buy the bed was to buy the whole estate, so he did. Built in the 1830s, the house was the hub of a thriving 2,400-acre corn and cotton plantation. Between 1858 and 1885, the plantation was the home of wealthy planter and merchant Arvah Hopkins, who turned Goodwood into a gathering place for Tallahassee high society, hosting elegant parties and balls in the grand southern style. Today, the house is open to the public and is superbly furnished with a truly remarkable collection of art and antiques.

Miccosukee Road winds for several miles out of the city, becoming more green and rural with every mile. The rolling hills are checkered with fields, meadows, woodlands, and the occasional horse farm. After turning onto Centerville Road, which is every bit as scenic as Miccosukee, you'll stop briefly to visit the tiny Pisgah United Methodist Church. Built in 1858, this is one of northern Florida's oldest churches.

Returning to Centerville Road, watch closely on your right for Bradley's Country Store, a working country store that has been providing the staples of everyday life to local residents and farmers since 1927. Bradley's, which is on the National Historic Register of Places, is not just a store, either; there is also a smokehouse on the premises where the Bradley family produces their legendary smoked country sausage. Beside the smokehouse, a ramshackle weathered shed is home to an ancient, belt-powered mill that grinds corn into grits and meal that is sold in the store—the store's originator, L. E. Bradley, built this mill house to grind corn for the area's farmers. Traditionally, Saturday was corn-grinding day, and farmers from all around would gather to have their corn ground into grits and meal and to swap stories and the news of the day. Not far from the mill house is a cane crusher used to process local ribbon sugar cane into cane syrup, a product that is still produced locally and carried in the store.

It is easy to blink and miss the community of Miccosukee, but you should make a point to stop here. It is one of the oldest

Crowns of gracious old live oaks form a green canopy over Pisgah Church Road, north of Tallahassee, Florida.

and most historic little settlements in the state, beginning as a native settlement in the eighteenth century. European encroachment and intertribal wars had pushed the Chiaha Creeks from their traditional lands in the Tennessee Valley into Georgia, and later northern Florida, where they associated with the Seminoles but remained separate, as they spoke their own dialect. At its height, the village contained sixty dwellings and twenty-eight extended families. In 1818, during the First Seminole War, Andrew Jackson marched across Florida, burning native villages; and the Miccosukee fled to the Everglades to join the Seminoles. Today, the tribe is thriving, owning casinos and other businesses throughout southern Florida. As for the village, it was slowly transformed by commercial enterprises of white settlers who established plantations throughout the area. In the mid- to late 1800s, the town prospered as an agricultural center with churches, schools, and a post office.

The boll weevil put an end to the cotton industry in this region, and Miccosukee, like many other small towns, faded, but the history of this quiet corner of the state remains fascinating.

A little farther on the route turns onto Magnolia Road, whose red dirt surface and sheltering green shade trees offer a glimpse of how Tallahassee's canopy roads may have looked a hundred years ago. A mile or so in, the road splits around the massive old "Dueling Oak" that has supposedly towered here since Andrew Jackson was in town.

Heading back to Tallahassee on SR 90, you can jump forward in time a couple of centuries and still be in the past at the Tallahassee Automobile Museum. This one-hundred-thousand-square-foot, award-winning facility displays over 140 antique and collectible autos, ranging from an 1894 Duryea to not one but three Batmobiles, all of which have appeared in television or movie versions of the Caped Crusader's story. The collection also includes an 1860 horse-drawn hearse that is believed to have carried Abraham Lincoln's body, a spectacular 1931 Duesenberg Model J, and numerous collections of Americana that range from baby bottles to Steinway pianos.

## 30

# GARDENS, BIRDS, and ANTIQUES

## TALLAHASSEE TO HAVANA

*From Tallahassee, take US Highway 319 north just past Interstate 10 to Maclay Road, and turn west (left). The entrance to the Alfred B. Maclay Gardens State Park is on the right. Return to Highway 319, and continue north to Bannerman Road/County Road 0342 and turn west (left). Continue on Bannerman Road to North Meridian Road/County Road 155 and turn north (right). County Road 155 crosses into Georgia; but there is no sign at the state line, so watch for a small sign that says Birdsong on the right, and turn in. Continue north on North Meridian Road to US Highway 319, and turn south (right) on Highway 319 to head into Florida. Turn west (right) on County Road 12, jogging briefly (right then left) as the road crosses North Meridian Road/County Road 155. Continue on County Road 12 to US Highway 27, and turn south (left) on Highway 27 into Havana.*

People are often surprised at the intensity of the green in the rolling hills of northwest Florida. One of the best places to appreciate this pastoral beauty is at the Maclay Gardens just north of downtown Tallahassee. Here, in 1923, financier Alfred B. Maclay built his winter home on the shores of Lake Hall. Tired of gray New York winters, Maclay wanted to be surrounded by beautiful gardens, and he set out to make his new Florida home a paradise of flowers and natural beauty. After his death, his wife continued with his vision, eventually donating their home to the state.

The gardens have spectacular collections of azaleas and camellias that come into peak bloom between January and May. Stone and brick footpaths lead through the elegant grounds to a charming lakeside gazebo that offers a spot to sit and contemplate the tranquil views. The gardens have also recently added almost nine hundred acres of gently undulating land, home to a variety of walking and biking trails.

True to its name, Meridian Road bisects Tallahassee on a north–south line before breaking ranks and wandering northeast into Georgia. North of the city, Meridian is one of Tallahassee's classic canopy roads and is a delight to drive. Towering oaks and other hardwoods create a sun-dappled tunnel of green over the road as it gently curves past small farms and fields.

There is no sign on this road to tell you that you have entered Georgia, but a farm with a large barn close to the

Left: Wildlflowers bloom along a roadside near Havana. In early spring, the fields and roadsides of northern Florida explode with painterly colors and textures of wildflowers.

Right: An ornate wrought-iron gate offers a peak into an inviting green nook of the Alfred B. Maclay Gardens State Park. Alfred and Louise Maclay began planting the gardens, which today encompass twenty-eight acres, in 1923.

road is a good place to start watching closely on your right for a very small sign that simply reads "Birdsong." This is the Birdsong Nature Center, open to the public on Wednesday, Friday, and Saturday from 9:00 a.m. to 5:00 p.m. and on Sunday from 1:00 p.m. to 5:00 p.m. In the mid-1800s, this land was part of a traditional cotton, tobacco, and vegetable farm typical of those found throughout northern Florida and southern Georgia.

Today, it is a quiet and lovely nature reserve whose groomed paths lead past woodlands, old farm fields, ponds, and wetlands that are home to more than 160 species of birds.

Birdsong was the life project of Ed and Betty Komarek. Ed was a biology major and Betty a teacher with a degree in botany when they discovered and purchased what was then a largely overgrown land and set about creating a wildlife study area and demonstration farm that became Birdsong. In their efforts, they cleared fields around the site and landscaped six acres of them to attract birds and wildlife.

The center of activity at Birdsong is the farmhouse, whose most striking feature is the wall-sized "bird window" that looks out on a charming, small garden that has been meticulously landscaped to attract birds with berry shrubs, fruit-bearing bushes, and feeders of

Above: **The pavilion at Alfred B. Maclay Gardens State Park offers a shady spot to sit and enjoy cool breezes coming across Lake Hall.**

Right: **Charming boutiques and specialty shops add color to historic downtown Havana, Florida. The town was once famous for its shade-grown tobacco, which was used to wrap cigars.**

all types. The centerpiece of the garden space is a small misty fountain that bubbles over boulders and into a pool carefully designed to allow birds of every size and shape to bathe. The window and garden were designed by Betty Komarek, who used it as a living teaching tool for the large tour groups that began coming to Birdsong in the 1950s and 1960s. So popular was this feature that she was asked to design similar bird windows for a variety of locations, including the famous Bok Sanctuary in Florida's Lake Wales.

Today, if you venture beyond the house, you can follow miles of paths that lead past weathered barns, through woodlands, and across gently rolling fields to a large pond and up to the Listening Place, a quiet screened hilltop shelter at the edge of a large meadow. Here, you can sit and listen to the sounds of nature—the frogs, crickets, cicadas, and, of course, the birds that flock here, just the way the Komareks envisioned they would when they started work on their dream almost seventy years ago.

From Birdsong, you'll make a lazy loop, first south back into Florida on US Highway 319, then west along County Road 12, which winds its way through a lush countryside of woodlands and horse farms, eventually arriving in the charming yesteryear village of Havana. The name of

An old barn stands in a sunlit meadow at Birdsong Nature Center. Renowned for its educational programs on the region's flora and fauna, the center is home to more than 160 species of birds.

this town is no accident. In the late 1800s and well into the twentieth century, this town was famous for growing shade-grown tobacco, whose leaves were used as the outer wrapper of cigars. True to its name, the tobacco was grown under shade netting supported by poles. Some of the tobacco was actually shipped to Cuba, while more made its way to the cigar factories of Tampa.

The shade-tobacco industry collapsed after 1950, and this little town slid into disrepair until 1984. That was the year that antique dealers Henderson and Lee Hotchkiss visited Havana looking for treasures. What they ended up buying instead was a block of rundown brick warehouses

that they lovingly refurbished, keeping one space for themselves and renting the rest to fellow antique-dealing friends. Over the next twenty years, they and the many store owners who followed have renovated almost all of the town's historic buildings.

Today, this town is a delightful place to stroll, shop, and dine. More than thirty specialty shops offer a large variety of antiques, collectibles, furniture, and gifts. Particularly worth a visit is Planters Exchange for antiques, collectibles, home accents, and gifts; and Wanderings, a store where owner Terri Paul displays international furniture, gifts, and handmade designer jewelry.

# 31

# SINKHOLES and BLUE SPRINGS

## TALLAHASSEE TO THE WAKULLA RIVER

*From Tallahassee, head south on US Highway 319 about five miles to the turnoff on the right side of the road into Leon Sinks Geological Area. After visiting the site, continue south on Highway 319 to State Road 267. Turn east (left) on Route 267 and continue to the entrance of Edward Ball Wakulla Springs State Park. Continue east on Route 267 to US Highway 98, then turn east (left) and go a short distance to Lighthouse Road. There, turn south (right) and continue on Lighthouse Road into St. Marks National Wildlife Refuge and on to St. Marks Lighthouse. Return to Highway 98 and turn west (left) to the intersection with State Route 363. Turn south (left) and go into the town of St. Marks. In St. Marks, turn right on Shell Island Road, then turn left on Fire Escape Road and continue on to San Marcos de Apalache Historic State Park. Return along Route 363 to Highway 98 and turn west (left) on Highway 98 and continue to the bridge over the Wakulla River. Watch just before the bridge for a left turn onto a river access/boat ramp side road and park at the kayak rental shop.*

Not far from downtown Tallahassee lies a sinkhole that serves as the front door to what scientists believe is the longest underwater cave system in North America—perhaps even the largest in the world. At Leon Sinks Geological Area, visitors can walk the 3.6-mile Sink Hole Trail, which leads through deep forest to several sinkholes, both the "wet" holes filled with ultraclear blue-green water and the fern-lined "dry" ones. An excellent viewing platform offers a close look down into the largest and prettiest of the sinks, known as Big Dismal Sink.

Big Dismal and the rest of the sinkholes here are really part of caves that formed as groundwater dissolved the limestone bedrock. As a cave eroded closer to the surface, the roof eventually collapsed, forming a sinkhole. Together, these sinkholes are part of a geologic region known as the Woodville Karst Plain, which stretches from Tallahassee to the Gulf of Mexico.

At Leon Sinks, several of these sinkholes lead to the maze of caves that extend laterally for many miles and are inhabited by many weird creatures, including albino crayfish, freshwater eels, and tiny shrimp-like creatures called amphipods. For several years, teams of highly trained divers, known collectively as the Woodville Karst Plain Project (WKPP), have been charting this cave system. The group's dives have included a record twenty-two-thousand-foot (4.1-mile) traverse, and members are credited with developing new technology for diver propulsion and

**Two exchange students examine the catch of a crab fisherman in Saint Marks National Wildlife Refuge.**

A boy does a back flip from the high-dive tower for the amusement of a tour boat full of visitors at Wakulla Springs State Park.

decompression that are being used worldwide. Recently, the WKPP divers discovered a tunnel connecting the Leon Sinks cave system with Wakulla Springs Cave over six miles away. The research at here is ongoing and helps scientists better understand the nature of limestone karst and the threatened Florida aquifer.

To visit the other end of this incredible cave system, just drive a few miles over to Wakulla Springs. The spring is one of the world's largest and deepest, spewing forth more than 250 million gallons of clear, pure water every day. Surrounded by six thousand acres of pristine forested state land, it has been here since well before the last ice age. Proof of this is evidenced by the vast numbers of bones of giant sloths, giant armadillos, camels, and other ice-age animals that litter the floor of the deep underwater cave that is the source of the spring. In fact, Wakulla Springs first came to national attention in 1850 when mastodon bones were discovered here.

In the late 1800s and early 1900s, the spring was a popular spot for picnics and family gatherings, and several owners attempted unsuccessfully to develop it into a tourist resort. In 1934, Edward Ball, brother-in-law of industrialist Alfred I. DuPont, purchased the site. He saw the potential for developing the area as an elegant retreat, and in 1937 he built the Wakulla Springs Lodge, which overlooks the spring. It was here that several of the Tarzan movies of the 1930s and 1940s starring Olympic swimmer Johnny Weissmuller were filmed. Wakulla Springs also doubled as the Amazon in the 1954 horror classic *Creature from the Black Lagoon*.

In spite of its colorful history of bones and creatures, this is a pleasant and relaxed setting. The spring is a sapphire and turquoise pool covering more than three acres and is surrounded by semitropical vegetation. This is also the ultimate swimming hole for both kids and adults, and it is hugely popular during the hot summers, as the water temperature stays a relatively constant and cool 70°F. It has a supervised and protected swim area (read: alligators on the outside of the net, swimmers on the inside) and a first-class diving tower. The small beach is a popular spot for sunbathing, and for parents to lounge while keeping an eye on the young ones.

Left: **A motorcyclist rides with his be-goggled canine partner along the backroads near St. Marks.**

Right: **Two fish out of water add a bright splash to an art gallery near Carrabelle, Florida.**

The other major attraction here is a glass-bottom boat tour that allows visitors to look down into the mouth of Wakulla Cave where the spring spews forth and to see the fossilized bones of Ice Age mammals on the river bed. A second, longer boat tour covers three miles of the river and focuses on wildlife, including eagles, fish, alligators, and the occasional manatee.

From Wakulla Springs, this route leads to St. Marks National Wildlife Refuge. This vast coastal wetland area encompasses sixty-eight thousand acres and was created in 1931 to provide habitat for migrating waterfowl. The leisurely five-mile drive from the park's entrance to the St. Marks Lighthouse is a visual treat. More than 250 species of birds visit here, with peak waterfowl migration in November and December; the park is also on the migratory path of the monarch butterflies, and tens of thousands of them pass through the area in October. The charming lighthouse was built here in 1832 and is still in operation today. Around the lighthouse are several easy walking trails that lead along the shore and past managed wetland ponds where waterfowl can be frequently seen.

Not far away, at the confluence of the Wakulla and St. Marks Rivers, is the town of St. Marks. In 1639, this strategic position did not escape the notice of the Spanish governor, who chose to build the fortress San Marcos de Apalache here, overlooking the junction of the two rivers. The site was not new to the Spanish; it had been visited by Panfilo de Narvaez in 1528 and by Hernando de Soto in 1539. However, the fort was only partly finished when the region was turned over to the British as booty from the war with Spain. Alas, no one really wanted this difficult area, and the Spanish gained control again in 1787.

Then, in 1818, after taking nearby Fort Gadsden, Andrew Jackson conquered this fort too, even though it was Spanish and no war had been declared between the United States and Spain. Jackson knew, however, that the Spanish had been harboring British agents, who had been arming the natives and inciting them to attack American settlements. Jackson tried and executed two British agents he found in the fort, which caused a major international incident. This act also helped make Spanish officials aware that they were unable to defend Florida, and three years later they ceded it to the United States. Today, the fort is a state historic site with a large interpretive center. Several paths lead to earthworks that stem from several periods in the fort's history. There are also peaceful benches that are shaded by ancient oaks that offer splendid views of the river.

A few miles from St. Marks, US Highway 98 crosses the Wakulla River. Watch closely for the bridge, as just before it, a gravel drive on the left leads to the river. This

Morning mist rises off the quiet waters of Wakulla Springs.

is the way to T-n-T Hide-a-Way canoe and kayak rentals, along the banks of the Wakulla River. Fed by the remarkably pure, cool waters of Wakulla Spring, the river flows with crystal clarity and is shrouded by tropical growth. If you have time, consider renting a kayak or canoe for a leisurely three-hour round trip upriver to Wakulla Springs State Park (the river is blocked at that point). If you're short on time, at least take a stroll along the bridge's pedestrian walkway to enjoy the views of this gorgeous river. Perhaps you can glimpse one of the manatees that have recently taken up residence here and are frequently seen feeding placidly on the water hyacinths below the bridge.

# INDEX

# ABOUT THE AUTHORS AND PHOTOGRAPHER

Paul Franklin has loved road trips since age twelve, when he rigged up a bicycle for overnight camping and headed out to explore the backroads of upstate New York.

Now a veteran travel photographer and writer, and often working with his wife and partner, Nancy Mikula, he has authored, coauthored and/or photographed sixteen travel guidebooks, including *The Barnes and Noble Complete Guide to the Public Parks and Gardens of Washington D.C.*, *Our Washington* (Voyageur Press), the *AAA Spiral Guide to Washington D.C.* and numerous DK Eyewitness and Top Ten Travel Guides including *The DK Eyewitness Travel Guide to Canada* and *The DK Eyewitness Travel Guide to the Southwest USA*, as well as *The Top 10 Guide to San Antonio* and *The Top 10 Guide to Mexico City*.

He has also participated in several recent large-format travel anthologies, including *National Geographic's 500 Journeys of a Lifetime*, *The World's Greatest Trips*, and DK's *Where to Go When: Best Destinations All Year 'Round*.

He authored and photographed *The DK Eyewitness Travel Family Guide to Washington D.C.*, which won the British Travel Press Award for Best Travel Guidebook of 2012. He is a member of the Society of American Travel Writers (SATW).

Nancy Mikula has a deep passion for travel and exploring along backroads to discover less-known and fascinating places.

She is the author of three books in the award-winning DK Top 10 Travel Guide series: *The Top 10 Guide to Santa Fe and Taos*, *The Top 10 Guide to San Antonio*, and *The Top 10 Guide to Mexico City*.

She has co-authored numerous books, including *The Eyewitness Travel Guide to Arizona and the Grand Canyon* and Voyageur Press's *Backroads of South Carolina* and *South Carolina's Plantations and Historic Homes*. She has also contributed to numerous guidebooks published by AAA, DK and Fodor's.

She has written numerous articles in large-format travel anthologies, including *National Geographic's Journeys of a Lifetime: 500 of The World's Greatest Trips*; *Sacred Places of a Lifetime: 500 of the World's Most Peaceful and Powerful Destinations*; *Secret Journeys of a Lifetime: 500 of the World's Best Hidden Travel Gems* and *DK Eyewitness Travel: Where to Go When*; and *Eyewitness Travel: The Americas Where to Go When: North, Central, South America and The Caribbean*. She is a member of the Society of American Travel Writers (SATW).